NORMAL'S JOURNEY

Mark H. Ballard

with

Timothy K. Christian

NORTHEASTERN BAPTIST PRESS

Normal's Journey
What Is the Gospel?
Copyright © 2021 by Mark H. Ballard & Timothy K. Christian

Published by Northeastern Baptist Press
Post Office Box 4600
Bennington, VT 05201

Paperback ISBN: 978-1-953331-03-8
ePub ISBN: 978-1-953331-04-5

To our children,

Benjamin Enoch Zhijang Ballard
Trina Maria Silva & Timothy Marcus Christian

Table of Contents

Foreword

There is a romantic aspect to the ministry. There is the challenge of preaching—sometimes to relatively large congregations, the challenge of taking the gospel to exotic places, the opportunity to lead in some ethical or moral emphasis much needed by the social order, and hundreds of other romantic adventures. But, every pastor knows that the "romance" of the ministry disappears rather quickly. There is an old adage about flying that says that "the business of flying is a matter of hours and hours of boredom punctuated by moments of stark terror." Such is also a reasonable assessment of the ministry. The moments of "stark terror" are actually moments that you crave if for no other reason than to break the boredom and the the humdrum of the daily ministry.

Any pastor, therefore, can identify with the story of *Normal's Journey*. Normal's name is felicitously chosen because the single character of this book is a normal human being with absolutely normal circumstances, a normal family, and a normal church relationship. Yet, for all the normality, Normal finds himself in a position of knowing that he is not really happy. Something is missing from his life and he cannot figure out what is missing.

While today Mark Ballard is a college president, he served many years as a pastor. Drawing upon his years of pastoral experience, Ballard has written in a sense the story of his pastoral ministry, literally to hundreds of people. A few along the line have been supernormal and not just one or two abnormal, but for the most part the people that the pastor deals with are unfailingly, well, normal! Often along the road these normal Christians seek a breakthrough to a more meaningful experience. The author of this book is well aware of the fact that too many Christians end up looking in the wrong place. Consequently, he has portrayed for us the magnificent discovery that this normal Christian makes, namely that the fulfillment of his dreams is found in his personal walk and relationship with Christ.

Every pastor will find his own ministry described in *Normal's Journey*. He may even find it to be a personal testimony of his own life. *Normal's Journey* is therefore the perfect gift to a believer who has reached that point in his Christian journey where he longs for something more profound than what he is experiencing in his day-by-day journey. This monograph could probably not have been written by someone other than a pastor or at least someone whose efforts to enhance the spiritual life of others are a front burner item.

The insights gained from the reading of this book will show the wisdom of years serving in a very secular society and yet faithfully ministering to the people of God in the midst of that society. The book has a thorough grasp of what really matters and what is peripheral, and that may be its greatest asset in the end. Whatever the case, *Normal's Journey* will be of infinite value to any pastor advising a saint who wants to experience the supernormal.

Paige Patterson
President
Sandy Creek Foundation
Dallas, TX

Part 1
THE JOURNEY

Chapter 1

THE INTRUDER

Like a nodding driver sideswiping a guardrail, Normal jerked awake. Something was wrong.

His bedside clock glowed 2:27.

What is it? What's wrong?

Normal checked the digital setting on his Sleep Number Bed. Fifty-one—his "ideal setting for maximum comfort."

Was it a dream? He didn't recall one.

Was it Average? He sensed her familiar, comfortable warmth.

In the darkness he listened with war-zone sentry intensity. The furnace murmured. Baseboard radiators clicked. The water softener's backwash activated at 2:30.

It's nothing. Go back to sleep.

Normal rolled over and adjusted. He snuggled close to Average. He was cozy and comfortable, but his eyelids wouldn't stay shut. A nagging feeling picked at his mind; then he knew.

Someone's broken in!

On high alert, the family protector slid from under the covers and into his slippers. Average didn't stir; she slept soundly, oblivious to the imminent danger. Normal moved through the darkness of their master suite. He felt for the doorknob, took a deep breath to steady his nerves, and eased the door open. His whole body was tense, ready to pounce on the intruder.

A single nightlight's soft glow barely illuminated the hallway. Even so, Normal determined it was empty. *Hallway clear*, he thought, and reminded himself to breathe.

Happy's bedroom door was ajar. Happy was their 15 year-old son. Moody's room was at the far end of the hall. As usual, their 17 year-old daughter's door was closed.

Like a special ops team-member, Normal crept down the hall. His slippers made a barely audible *scrinch* on the wool Berber carpet. He hoped the intruder couldn't hear it.

Normal checked Happy's room and bath—no one hiding in the shower. *Clear.*

Happy slept soundly and … happily. In spite of the funky teenage boy aroma, all was well.

Normal checked Moody's door. Locked. As expected. He pressed his ear against the door but heard nothing. Moody was safe.

He checked the guest suite and bath. *Clear*. At least the intruder had not made it to the second floor.

Normal paused at the top of the stairs to listen. Silence.

He made a quick assessment. *If this is a robbery, the intruder's experienced. He's working quietly. If it's a home invasion, he may be hiding. Either way, I'll take him by surprise. He's on my turf.*

Normal moved down the stairs, clearing the last two with a leap. Landing at the front door, he checked the locks. "Secure," he whispered. He imagined an earpiece in his right ear and a sub-vocalization microphone at the base of his throat. Normal had definitely been filling his action movie quota.

Normal turned to his left, leaned against the wall and peeked in before entering the living room. Cautiously, he checked beside and behind each piece of furniture. "Living room secure," he whispered. "Checking the family room and kitchen."

LED lights on various kitchen appliances cast a faint, irregular, eerie green light onto the kitchen floor. The family room, however, was mostly in shadows. A quick dart in and check around the furniture revealed nothing amiss, but he had to check for the intruder crouching behind the kitchen bar. Normal crawled covertly from the couch to the corner of the bar and quick-peeked, nose and eyeball, around the bar.

Relief. *Family room and kitchen clear. Moving into the dining room next.*

He eased back behind the bar to breathe, gather his nerves, and message a cramp in his left thigh. And that was when ... a stack of junk mail poured onto his head and into his lap. He had jostled the barstool where it was stacked.

Normal choked back a scream. He tried to calm himself. *Breathe. Control your bladder. You're not under attack.* The pep talk helped a little, but very little. His heart was pounding. He was nearing hyperventilation, but he knew he had to complete his mission.

With a trembling hand he pushed the mail aside and steeled himself to investigate the dining room. The family was counting on him. At least they would be if they were awake and aware of their peril.

The dining room was a bit darker than the other rooms on the ground floor. Milky light from a streetlamp formed gray shadows near a drapery and sheer-covered window. The rest of the dining room stood dark, except for a tiny green light glowing in the smoke detector on the ceiling.

Normal took a couple of deep breaths and prepared to spring through the dining room door.

Go! Go! Go!

A summersault through the door sailed Normal's right slipper into the darkness beside the dining room table. *Equipment malfunction! Repairs in progress.*

Normal crawled beside the table, groping for his slipper in the darkness. When he found it and slipped it on, he stood in a crouched, wrestler's position—feet spread, knees bent, arms chest high, hands ready. He pivoted to his left, searching the shadows. And froze.

In horror, Normal stared into a pair of large, cruel eyes, only inches away.

The features were difficult to distinguish, but Normal could see the intruder was huge. He was also ugly—hideously ugly. His eyes bulged in distorted features. Obviously he had been in multiple disfiguring prison fights.

Normal would have run from the room screaming, but panic cemented his feet to the floor. It choked his larynx.

Somewhere he had heard advice for such a situation. Shock your intruder into submission with a sharply spoken, authoritative question, "What are you doing here!" He tried but it didn't come out exactly that way.

"Whump," he whimpered. "Guu-lk."

Normal's heart galloped out of control. Perspiration popped out on his face and neck and trickled down his back. A large drop of sweat dripped from the end of his nose. He stared into the horrifying, unblinking eyes.

Normal tried to swallow. It was hard to breathe. He had to do something.

Quick! Jab his eyes; now or never! Normal's panic-stiffened arm responded with an awkward wave.

The vicious, escaped prisoner waved back.

Distorted features softened as Normal's eyes adjusted. Normal blinked. The intruder blinked. Normal lowered his trembling hands. So did the intruder.

He was neither as big nor as ugly as Normal initially thought. In fact, he was quite handsome for being up so late. Normal moved the decorative bowl aside so he could see his whole face in the mirror of Average's china cabinet.

Normal stood on Jell-O legs and breathed the sweet air of the rescued. He wiped his face and neck on the tail of his damp t-shirt.

Normal continued checking the first floor, but he knew all was safe. The bathroom and laundry room were secure. The windows and doors were locked and unbroken. He checked the three-car garage. He checked the man cave, guest suite, and family/game room in the basement. All was safe.

Yet, the gnawing feeling didn't go away. Something *was* wrong.

Chapter 2

THE SYMPTOM

The lamp clicked and Normal sank into his overstuffed leather recliner. For a few minutes he stared at his feet and the blank television screen.

At 3:17 it hit him. *I'm having one of Grandma's premonitions. It must be hereditary.* He grabbed the remote control to his high definition flat-screen and checked all the news channels.

"Nothing," he said aloud. "I just don't get it."

Normal reclined in his chair. He tried, but could not sleep. Neither could he understand his persistent uneasiness. At 6:07 he heard the shower in the master bath. Average was up. Preparation for another day was under way.

Everyone getting up and showered, fed and out the door on time, was a challenge on a good day. Average, Moody, and Happy were on schedule, but for Normal, this was not a good day. He managed to get out of the house 10 minutes late, and just in time to see the railroad crossing arms come down a couple of blocks from his driveway. Normal counted 2 locomotives, 137 freight cars, and a caboose. It wasn't little or red.

All day the mysterious, haunting, troubled feeling clung to Normal like a cloud to a mountaintop. He avoided people as much as possible, but his associates noticed. He was distant and disconnected. He wasn't acting normal.

The boss noticed his lethargic demeanor when he returned from lunch. Normal had not actually eaten lunch. He sat in his car with the key in his hand until he noticed it was time to be back in the office. When he shuffled in, the boss said, "Norm, is everything OK?"

"Transfer the call. I'll see what he wants," Normal said. He ambled to his office without looking back.

At dinner, Average and Happy noticed Dad's somber mood. Each tried to start a conversation. He answered questions with a grunt. He alternated between staring at the wall and at his plate. Occasionally he groaned, moved some food around on his plate, sipped his water and returned to his silent stares. And so it continued day after day.

Weeks of confusion became months of despair. Normal's certainty of an unspecified, drastic problem grew. Even Moody noticed.

Friends encouraged him to talk. Family members offered advice. Normal's church added him to the prayer list. His Men's Bible Study group felt sorry for him, at least for a while. As time wore on, their sympathy turned toward Average, Happy, and Moody.

Pastor Goodman tried. Normal knew his counsel was impractical and a little simplistic. He was stuck on the idea that Normal's problem was actually a spiritual longing. Normal knew he meant well.

After repeated urging (or was it nagging?), Normal made an appointment with Dr. Phil Good, a local Psychiatrist. Dr. Good ordered a complete physical.

"Everything checks out fine." Dr. Phil Good was looking at Normal's lab report. "Physically, you're in great shape." He looked up from the chart.

"Psychologically and emotionally, we need to do some work. I'm concerned about clinical depression, but let's not start with medication. Let's start with eight weeks of Feel-Good therapy sessions."

Dr. Good smiled and spoke in a cheerful, positive tone. "We'll break through your cloud. Trust me. It's my specialty. It won't be long before you start to feel good."

For the eight weeks, Normal was a model patient. He never missed a session or a co-pay. His company insurance paid on time. He was open and honest with Dr. Good, and a time or two thought he had made a breakthrough.

Each week he left with a "Phil Good Funny" and a "Feel-Good Phrase" to repeat. But he didn't start to feel good. The cloud remained and darkened.

Dr. Good officially diagnosed clinical depression and prescribed a mood-altering medication. Normal took it for a month. It didn't take away the cloud; it put him in a drowsy fog. Normal wanted to feel better, not numb. He preferred feeling something was wrong to feeling nothing at all. He refused to drowse his life away.

The three-month effort ended in disappointment. Normal declined a medication change, and canceled his standing appointment with "Dr. Phil Good, the Feel-Good Specialist."

Normal, however, could not cancel the gnawing feeling inside. No one could talk, counsel, console, cajole, or medicate his cloud away. Then, one day while sitting in his leather recliner, staring at the blank television screen, he had a simple, profound realization. "I'm dissatisfied," Normal said aloud. "That's it. That's the gnawing feeling!"

But why? Average is pleasant, attractive, and in my book, above average. Our teenagers haven't given us any reasons to worry. They aren't in trouble at school. They make passing grades. They're active in the church youth program. We love them and they love us. I like my job. We built our dream-home. Our car is comfortable, safe, and gets good gas mileage. I have a nice truck and more "big boy" toys than I ever dreamed possible. I go to church and Bible study. I'm more involved than the average church member and I know I'm on my way to heaven. I have ev-

erything a man could ask for, so why am I dissatisfied? It
makes no sense.

Normal had identified his gnawing feeling, but now he had a new problem. Dissatisfaction was the symptom, but its source remained a mystery. Still, knowing the symptom gave him a little hope. If he could discover why he was dissatisfied, maybe he could find satisfaction again. Maybe he could return to being the old Normal. Small hope trumps no hope every time.

Chapter 3

THE ANNOUNCEMENT

"What's up?" Happy asked. "Why are we eating in the dining room? I thought it was reserved for company and holidays."

"I'm not sure. Dad wants us to eat in here," Average said, as she placed a steaming bowl of green beans on the table. "He said he has an announcement."

"What announcement?" Happy asked.

"I knew it," Moody said. "Dad has a brain tumor." She sat and buried her face in her hands.

Normal entered the dining room in a less spectacular fashion than on a previous occasion. He set a basket of rolls and a plate of roast beef on the table.

Moody, fighting back tears, asked, "Is it malignant? Are you dying? How much time do they think you have? Tell me the truth."

"Hold on. Nothing so dramatic. This is a family celebration," Normal laughed. "I have good news. Happy, pray for us, and we'll eat while it's hot."

They bowed their heads and Happy prayed, "Thanks a lot God. Looks like some good groceries. In Jesus' name, Amen."

"Short and to the point," Normal said with his first genuine smile in months. "Please pass the beans."

As they served their plates, Normal proceeded with his announcement. "First, I owe you an apology." Normal looked each of them in the eye as he spoke. "I haven't been myself for the last few months. That's not an excuse. It's a fact. You know it better than anyone."

Normal hoped someone would speak up: "Don't worry Dad; it's not been so bad. That's Ok, honey. No need to apologize." But no one even grunted. Average nodded in agreement. So, with a bit less enthusiasm, he continued.

"I've been gloomy and distant. I haven't been here when you needed me. My dark cloud affected my reasoning; I see that now. I don't know what I was thinking when I gave you cemetery plots for Christmas. I'm truly sorry. But things are about to change. At last I've figured out my problem."

For Normal, the announcement was monumental. He was holding the meat fork in his left hand. A small piece of meat was speared on the end of the two long, narrow tongs. He gestured dramatically with the knife in his right hand as he announced, "Dissatisfaction. That's my problem. I'm dissatisfied."

Normal wasn't sure what response he had expected. He'd hoped for more than the shocked, silent, blank stares he saw before him.

Average was the first to break the uncomfortable silence. "Are you planning to quit your job, or ... leave us?"

"Of course not. That never crossed my mind."

"Ooo-kay." Average was hesitant. "Why are you dissatisfied?"

"I don't ... well ... I ... uh ... haven't figured that part out yet. I just know I'm dissatisfied."

Happy said, "Great. Now we can get back to normal. I mean, Dad, you've been a real buzz-kill lately. It's been like having two Moody's in the house. That's too much for anybody."

Moody ignored Happy and patted Normal's hand sympathetically. "I understand, Dad. Half the time, I don't know why I feel the way I do, either." She looked at her mother and brother, then back to her dad. "I think some good can come out of the last few months. For one thing, I've learned that you have feelings, Dad. I never thought about that before. But most important, now that things are going back to normal, I think you'll be able to understand me a little better." She glanced back to Average and Happy while continuing to pat her dad's hand. "In fact, I think this family experience will help everyone be more considerate of my feelings."

Happy grinned at Moody. "What a relief. For a few minutes there I was worried this wasn't all about you."

Moody rolled her eyes.

"I'm not sure you understood my point," Normal said, looking around the table. "I love you; I like my job. None of that's changed. But something inside me is different. For the past few months I've had a nagging, dreadful feeling that something is wrong. Just yesterday I realized I'm dissatisfied. It was like a light came on. I can't explain it yet, but now I know what to work on. So pray for me, and try to be patient a little longer. I'm going to do all I can to figure out why I'm dissatisfied. Ask God to show me what it is."

Chapter 4

THE CABIN

For the first time in seven months Normal was hopeful. Nothing had changed, yet everything had changed. Something was still wrong, but at least he knew why—he was dissatisfied deep inside.

Normal decided to take a step-by-step approach to discovering why he was dissatisfied. He spent Saturday afternoon formulating a plan. He knew he couldn't approach his problem exactly like a work project. He wouldn't have a team of associates or a company-funded budget at his disposal, but he could take a methodical approach to discovering why he was dissatisfied. After a Google search for "steps to problem-solving," he chose an easy to follow, 7-step plan. The suggested steps were:

1. Identify the problem
2. Define the problem

3. Form a strategy
4. Organize information
5. Allocate resources
6. Monitor progress
7. Evaluate the results[1]

Normal's high hopes fizzled quickly. He lacked the strategic information needed to move beyond step one. Dissatisfaction was not his problem. It was only a symptom. He couldn't define the problem, form a strategy, or organize information until he identified the root cause.

What can I do? Normal thought. *Without a personal epiphany, I may be dissatisfied for the rest my life. Lord Jesus, help me. Show me why I'm dissatisfied.* His desperation was growing again.

Normal decided to ask for a personal day the following Friday. He would go to their mountain cabin for the day or for the weekend. If necessary, he would take some vacation days the following week. He was determined to stay until he discovered the reason for his dissatisfaction.

After clearing the time off with his boss, Normal could hardly wait for Friday to arrive. He felt like a 10 year-old waiting for Christmas morning. On Thursday night he packed some personal items in his gym bag. He put in a few toiletries (just in case of an extended stay),

---

1. "What Is Problem-Solving?" (accessed 1 February 2016); available from http://psychology.about.com/od/problem-solving/f/problem-solving-steps.htm.

underwear and socks, a couple of knit shirts, and a new Northeastern Baptist College sweatshirt (Moody was headed to Bennington, Vermont for the fall semester). He also took his Kindle Fire© with its charger.

Before daybreak on Friday, Normal picked up breakfast at a fast food drive-thru and headed into the mountains. He had a great sense of anticipation. *Maybe today will be the day*.

Traffic was light. Normal listened to his favorite praise-music and savored his coffee as he drove the familiar mountain roads on mental autopilot. He arrived at his log cabin almost before he realized it. The early morning sun peeked into the secluded mountain ravine.

Normal placed his bag inside the cabin, lit the fire, and stepped back onto the porch to breathe the fresh air and take in the view. The clear sky promised a beautiful spring day. A rambling, swollen stream was visible through the budding trees some 30 yards down the hill. Warmer days and April showers had melted the snow into spotty patches. Beyond the stream, the tree covered mountainside rose to a ridge. Normal and his family had hiked to the top many times. The panoramic view of a mountain lake and the Presidential Range beyond always rewarded the effort.

Normal's attention turned toward the top of the ridge. He could hear hunting dogs baying faintly in the distance. *This isn't hunting season. They must have escaped*. At that moment, a medium-sized deer bounded over the ridge and down to the stream. Normal could see his sides heaving. It drank deeply before looking back toward the sound of the hounds. After another quick drink, it leaped the swollen brook, and raced past Normal's truck and out of sight.

The hounds were coming closer. It reminded Normal of the chorus he'd heard a few minutes before pulling up to the cabin.

> As the deer pants for the water,
> So my soul longs after You.
> You alone are my heart's desire,
> And I long to worship You.[2]

"Enough of that," Normal said. "Don't get distracted with deer and dogs and a chorus. Don't forget why you're here. Today is the day."

With that personal pep talk, he entered the cozy cabin and went to work at a rustic table near the fireplace. *I'll start with a list of possibilities for my dissatisfaction.* He opened the notepad on his Kindle and typed:

> Faith
> Family

Just then the dogs came baying up to the cabin. Through a window Normal could see five or six black and tan hounds waging their tails, sniffing and circling his

---

2. Martin Nystrom, "As The Deer," (Maranatha! Music, 1984); accessed Feb. 10, 2016, http://www.higherpraise.com.

truck, watering the tires. *Should I see if the owner's name is on their collars? Maybe give him a call?*

Momentarily, one of the hounds regained the trail and the pack was back in business. *That answers the question.*

As the deer pants for the water, so my soul longs after You. You alone are my heart's desire . . . Normal stopped himself. *Stay on task. I'll never find satisfaction if I spend the morning singing.* He refocused on listing possible sources of his dissatisfaction and added:

Friends
Health
Job
House
Vehicles
Retirement

"That's a start," Normal said. "Maybe the problem's here somewhere." He reviewed the list, but couldn't decide where to start. Each time he focused on one issue, his eyes and thoughts wandered to another.

Normal decided to turn each word into a separate page and focus on one at a time. He scrolled back to the first page.

Faith

"Am I dissatisfied with my faith?" he asked aloud. "That's not a tough question; it's a dangerous question. How could I be dissatisfied with God?"

After thinking it over for a moment he said, "Of course, there's a difference between God and my faith in God. Maybe my faith is faulty."

"How can I answer? I guess, start at the beginning." Normal wrote:

> I grew up in a Christian home. Perfect? No. What home is? Dad and Mom did their best; I never questioned their love. We had a good home. They taught me Bible stories from as early as I can remember. We went to church two or three times a week.
>
> <u>First major spiritual crisis.</u> I was 10. I discovered my biggest problem: I'm a sinner and God punishes sin. The punishment for sin is separation from God—forever—in hell. That frightened me. It kept me awake at night.
>
> Out of desperation, I finally told Dad why I wasn't sleeping very well.
>
> "I'm glad," Dad said with a smile.
>
> That hurt my feelings. How could my Dad be happy that I was worried and afraid?
>
> He explained. "Some people worry about stuff they can't do anything about. Your problem has a solution. God solved it a long time ago. He sent His Son, Jesus Christ

to earth. He was God in a human body. He lived a perfect life; He never sinned. But do you remember what happened to Him?"

"Sure Dad," I said. "We learned that in Sunday school. People said Jesus was bad when He was really good. They crucified Him and He didn't even try to stop them. They made fun of Him and told Him they'd believe if He came down from the cross. I wish He had. I wish He would've shown them what He could do."

"I used to think the same thing," Dad said, "but I'm glad He didn't. When Jesus died on the cross, He was punished for everyone's sins. The Bible says, 'The wages of sin is death.' Sin has a death penalty. Normal, you earned the death penalty."

"But, Jesus died in our place. He died for Mom's sins, our sins, and the sin of everyone in the whole world. Jesus didn't sin, but He stayed on the cross. He was punished for all of our sins. Now, you don't have to be punished. You can trust Jesus to take away your sin."

"The Bible says, 'Whoever calls on the name of the Lord shall be saved.' Normal, you can receive Jesus as your Savior and you won't have to worry about hell anymore. You will be on your way to heaven."

Dad asked if I wanted to receive Jesus. I had heard it all before. But Jesus' death on the cross, the garden tomb, and His resurrection seemed like a story for people long ago and far away. I never doubted it was true; I just never thought about it meaning anything to me. That night was different.

I knew I was a sinner, but Jesus died for me. I prayed with Dad. I trusted Jesus Christ as my Savior. Instantly I knew something had changed inside me. I had peace. My fear was gone.

The next Sunday, Mom walked forward with me when Pastor Wise gave an invitation at the end of his sermon. I was scared, but excited. I wanted everyone to know that Jesus saved me.

I was baptized two weeks later. Spiritual growth was easy and natural. I developed the habit of daily prayer and Bible reading. Pastor Wise told me I was supposed to, so I did.

Everything seemed to click. I prayed for my school friends, and invited them to attend church with me. I took Ben, Blake, Cindy, and Tyrone to Vacation Bible School. All four of them trusted Jesus that week. Those were happy days; I knew God was working in my life and had a great plan for me.

Why don't I feel that way now? If God had an answer for my biggest problem (nothing's bigger than an eternal problem), why doesn't He give me an answer now? Does it have anything to do with what happened to me in college? Normal continued writing.

Second major spiritual crisis. I drifted
spiritually while in college, though I began
with better intentions. During my freshman
year I attended a Bible study at the Baptist
Student Center from time to time. I was in-
consistent. I didn't get involved. I also attended a local church most Sunday mornings. There was a college group, but again, I
didn't attend.

Things changed sophomore year. My
roommates were upper classmen. Newton
was an astronomy major, and Charles was
pre-med. After they joked about Christians
who believed in God and denied evolution,
I was intimidated. How could a business major defend his beliefs against science majors?
I didn't want them to see my Bible, much
less see me read it. After I slept in a couple of Sunday mornings and lightning didn't
strike me, sleeping in on Sunday got pretty
easy. Prayer was reserved for exams. I drifted away from my prayer and Bible reading
habit. My church attendance became incon-
sistent and sporadic.

But I didn't go the typical route of
all-out rebellion. I was better behaved than
the other men on my dorm floor.

Wait a minute. Does that matter? Is it self-justifying?

I'm glad I don't have a bunch of baggage to feel guilty about, but does that make

me better than anyone else? I wasn't close to Jesus; I was ashamed of Him. By my senior year I didn't want anyone in the dorm to know I was a Christian.

I don't have any reason to congratulate myself. My faith became secondary where it had been primary. That was a different kind of rebellion, but it was rebellion just the same.

Forgive me Jesus. I've never thought of it that way before. I didn't realize what I was doing.

Am I doing any better now? I thought I was until recently. For the past few months, as I asked God to show me what's wrong, He didn't answer. I can't remember an answered prayer in a long time. I never thought about it until I needed something I couldn't buy.

Has my religion become church activity without much going on inside? Maybe that's what Pastor Goodman means when he talks about people having "churchianity" instead of Christianity.

Lately, since I re-started regular Bible reading and prayer, it's becoming meaningful again. The pastor's sermons and the adult Bible Study lessons have taken on new meaning. I've been praying about my dissatisfaction. Maybe God is answering but I don't know how to listen.

I'm getting off track again. Stick to the plan. Normal wrote:

Toward the end of my senior year of college, I started thinking about my relationship with God again. I wanted to go in a new direction. Graduation seemed like a good opportunity. I asked God for a good job in a good place to live. I promised to start a new chapter in my life. I promised to find a Christ-centered, Bible-preaching church and be an involved member.

I kept that promise. I found the church and met Average. I'm glad we've raised Moody and Happy in a healthy church with a faithful, long-term pastor. His preaching and leadership have impacted our family.

Pastor Goodman often says, "Every believer should be involved in at least one worship service, one small group, and one ministry every week. It's three healthy steps in spiritual growth."

I'm doing more than his 1+1+1 standard. We go to Sunday school and church on Sunday morning and attend the prayer service most Wednesday evenings. I'm involved in Men's Bible Study once a month. I enjoy the small group interaction with other guys. I'm on the building and grounds ministry team, and I tithe. I serve and give more than most. I'm doing everything I know to do, short of going into the ministry or to the mission field.

Pastor Goodman's counsel that my feeling of something being wrong was the sign of a deeper spiritual need couldn't be right. Could it?

Despite some growing questions, Normal thought his faith was an asset. It couldn't be causing his dissatisfaction. He moved on to the next page.

Family

My relationships with my parents, in-laws, grandparents, and extended family members are fine. I had a secure, happy childhood. Nothing unusual. No baggage there.

I met Average in the College and Career Sunday School class. We dated for three months before I proposed. By our third date, I knew I had found the love of my life. At the time, our six-month engagement seemed a lot longer than it was. Anticipation and excitement made time crawl. Anyway, we had a beautiful wedding with a beautiful bride. Our awesome honeymoon was the doorway into a wonderful life.

I'm sounding like a Hallmark movie advertisement. No one else will see this. I can be honest with myself. Am I dissatisfied with my wife or children? Is there something I don't want to admit to myself?

Average: In nearly 20 years of marriage, like everyone else, we've had ups and downs. Our marriage hasn't been perfect, but plenty of people would be happy to live in our shoes. As Pastor Goodman says, "We've been blessed—we've enjoyed God's supernatural favor." Most of the time, at least until the last several months, we've been happy and comfortable with one another.

I admit I haven't been good company since early last September. Average has endured more than her share of frustration with me. She's been patient. She wanted to understand, but I've been moodier than Moody. I pushed her away when she wanted to comfort me. Over and over she asked me to explain my feelings, but I couldn't. The question frustrated me. I was angry with myself, but sometimes I responded as if it was her fault.

What am I doing to Average? Her first thought after my big announcement was to ask if I was leaving. It makes sense. I've been grumpy while Average has been supportive. She's been about the best thing that's ever happened to me.

I have to let her know that before I wound our marriage more than I already have. Average isn't my source of dissatisfaction.

Moody: What can I say about my little girl? She's the second love of my life. She was born 17 months after we married. At times I wished we had waited to have children. I wanted to have Average to myself a little longer. Now that Moody is 18, I'm glad we didn't wait. She entered the difficult teen years when she was about 7, but really, she hasn't given us grief or worry. Even though she tends to be moody and self-absorbed, she's becoming a beautiful young woman. I'm proud of her. We'll miss her when she's away at college, but I think she's ready for the next stage in her life. She's been growing spiritually. I'm glad she picked Northeastern Baptist College in Vermont. It will encourage her faith rather than destroy her faith.

Happy: Born 22 months after Moody, Happy is Mr. Personality. Since his birth he's been able to put a smile on my face. His positive outlook is contagious. Happy encourages the whole family. In recent months, when I've been obsessed with my deep dissatisfaction, (but not knowing I was dissatisfied), Happy was one of the few who could lift my spirits. Temporarily. The only time I've worried about Happy was a couple of months back when he got his license and started driving alone.

I need to find satisfaction again so that I can reconnect with my son. He said I've been a "buzz-kill." Good description. He

told me the dark truth, and gave me a smile
at the same time.

Normal had discovered new motivation for solv-
ing the puzzle of his dissatisfaction. In fact, he suddenly
realized it was more urgent than he'd thought. Even so,
as far as he could tell, he was no closer to an answer.
He felt like a person trying to work a crossword puzzle
without any clues.

"The problem isn't my family," Normal said, "but I
may be my family's problem." He advanced to the next
page.

Friends

Normal looked at the heading and remembered
a Sunday morning service a few months back. Pastor
Goodman had said, "A true friend is a rare find." At the
time, it struck his heart like an arrow. Normal wasn't
sure why, but it made him uncomfortable. He remembered thinking; *I'm trying to get rid of my "something is
wrong" feeling. I don't need anything else cluttering my
conscience.*

Normal had spent the rest of the service trying to
push the thought out of his mind. Now he wished he
had listened. He wondered if his pastor had described a
true friend or explained how to find a true friend.

Thinking back, that was an odd response. Why was I bothered by friendship? Friends are good. He decided to write a few notes.

> I have friends, good friends—friends at work, at church, in the neighborhood. But do I have a true friend?
>
> Typical is a good friend. We enjoy occasional fishing trips. Next to Average, he may be my best friend. But, is Typical a true friend? What is a true friend?

Normal opened the Bible on his Kindle and searched for the word "friend." He discovered that the words "friend," "friends," and "friendly" are used 113 times in 105 Bible verses. "Friendship" is used twice. A couple of ideas caught his attention as he read. He was surprised the two "friendship" verses are warnings. After an hour of reading verses and meditating on the meaning of different phrases, Normal wrote:

> Some people are bad friends. Avoid their friendship. "Make no friendship with an angry man, and with a furious man do not go, lest you learn his ways and set a snare for your soul" (Prov. 22:24-25). A friend's character rubs off on me—bad or good. Choose wisely! A true friend's character will make me a better man.
>
> The world is a dangerous friend. "Adulterers and adulteresses! Do you not know that friendship with the world is en-

mity with God? Whoever therefore wants to be a friend of the world makes himself an enemy of God" (James 4:4). I don't want to be God's enemy.

A true friend will enhance my friendship with God and discourage my friendship with the world. A true friend has Godly character. A false friend encourages spiritual adultery. Wow! That's harsh.

How can I make a true friend? Maybe Proverbs 18:24 answers the question. "A man who has friends must himself be friendly, but there is a friend who sticks closer than a brother." It makes sense. Friendly people make friends. Unfriendly people don't.

I'm doing OK. I have friends and I am pretty friendly, at least I was until the last few months. Overall, I think I'm a friendly guy.

But the second half of the verse stumps me. "There is a friend who sticks closer than a brother." A true friend is a closer-than-a-brother friend. The friend knows me for who I am, accepts me as I am, but encourages me not to stay as I am. A true friend is a life transformer.

Typical doesn't fit that description.

Normal spent the next hour thinking about his friendships. He wondered if those he called "friends" were better because they associate with him. "About all I've had to offer these days is gloom."

He couldn't think of a friendship with another man that had consistently enhanced his relationship with God and made him a better man. A few had the opposite effect.

On the negative side, Normal remembered his college roommates, Newton and Charles. On the positive side, he thought of the guys in his Men's Bible Study. They encouraged him, but he was seldom transparent with them.

Finally, Normal concluded that he had lots of acquaintances but he had never had a true friend. He doubted he had ever been a true friend.

Normal realized he had issues with friendship, but he didn't know what to do about it. He decided to move on to the next page.

Health

Normal was as confident about his physical health as anyone could be. His emotional health was a different issue. That's why he was here in the cabin. Since he had always been diligent about his physical health, and had no answers for his emotional health, he wrote a quick note.

I eat a healthy diet, exercise, take vitamins, and have regular check-ups. Dr. M. Dee gave me a clean bill of health after my annual check-up last June. Dr. Phil Good's prescribed physical in October yielded the same result. I'm confident my dissatisfaction isn't connected with physical health.

Thinking of his health called attention to his stiff back and numb seat. The rustic-wood chair certainly wasn't ergonomic. It was 1:30 in the afternoon. He decided to charge his Kindle while he stretched his legs with a walk around the cabin. The morning's search had given him plenty to think about. Some fresh air would do him good.

Chapter 5

THE HIKE

Normal returned from his hike, deep in thought, and more than a little shaken.

The hike was exceptional. He intended only to stretch his legs and rest his back. When he reached the edge of the clearing around the cabin, he walked a little further into the forest. Having gone that far, he decided to walk to the old logging trail that led to the top of the ridge. Having reached the trail, he decided to walk up the next bend in the trail. As he walked and breathed the fresh mountain air, intending to walk just a bit further, he began to give thanks and pray and sing praise choruses. He surprised himself; this wasn't His usual practice.

Generally, Normal was the unemotional type. Today, the surrounding beauty stirred his emotions; joy and gratitude erupted within. *This isn't an accident of mindless natural forces! This is the intricate handiwork of the all-wise, all-powerful Creator.*[1]

The welcome spring sunshine warmed his shoulders and ears. It was melting the few remaining snow patches. Normal unzipped his ski vest and stuffed his fur-lined gloves into his pockets. The sky was a brilliant blue. A green sheen of buds was visible on the part of the mountainside that was warmed by the morning and mid-day sun. Majestic evergreen spruce trees were generously sprinkled among the maple, birch, and oak trees.

Yeah, God. Good job of creation. The heavens really do declare Your glory,[2] *and so does this beautiful mountainside.*[3]

Before he realized it, Normal was at the top of the ridge. He looked into the valley on the other side. He could see a mountain lake and the ridges beyond. From his vantage point, he could see for miles. One of the songs he heard on the drive up came to mind.

Shout to the Lord, all the earth let us sing,
Power and majesty, praise to the King!
Mountains bow down and the seas will roar,
At the sound of your name!
I sing for joy at the work of your hands,
Forever I'll love you; forever I'll stand,

---

1. Romans 1:20
2. Psalm 19:1
3. Psalm 65:6

Nothing compares to the promise I have in You.[4]

Singing and praying, as he took in the view, sent him to his knees in worship. At that moment, it seemed to be the uncharacteristically normal thing to do.

Soon Normal was on his face, overwhelmed by how small and insignificant he truly was compared to the grandeur around him. "Lord Jesus, You made and maintain all of this.[5] How can it be that You have time to think of me, to hear my prayers, to know my thoughts, to care for my needs?[6] ... But You do. You know me[7] ... and love me. You came to die for me[8] and now You live in me! How can it be?"

Normal was overcome by the reality of God's transcendence, yet equally aware of God's tender love and nearness. He felt compelled to bow as low as possible. What else can one do in HIS presence? He continued to pray.

But lying prostrate, face down, didn't seem low enough. He pushed thawed leaves aside, dug a small hole with his finger and pressed his nose into the soil. "Father, I don't know how to get any lower. Please, though I don't deserve it, in Jesus name, forgive me. Wash me. I confess my sins. Cleanse me with Jesus' blood. Until this moment, I've never realized how truly

---

4. Michael W. Smith
5. John 1:3; Colossians 1:16-17
6. Psalm 8:3-4; Matthew 10:30
7. Psalm 139:1-4
8. John 3:16

unworthy I am." He covered his head with damp leaves. He didn't know what else to do.

"Father, help me," Normal sobbed aloud. "I've been unsatisfied and miserable for months, but I don't know why. Please ... Please! Show me." He cried out the prayer again and again. Though he had not shed a tear in years, now it was as if a dam had broken in his soul.

The damp, woody aroma filled his nostrils. Something tickled the side of his nose. Instinctively he jerked his head up and looked. It was green sprig of grass, sprouted beneath the leaves. Tears dripped onto the soil as he looked at the single, tiny blade of grass.

He placed his nose back in the little hole. "That's what I need Jesus. Just as You created new grass to grow in the spring, I need new life in my barren soul. Thaw my cold heart."[9]

He wasn't sure how long he lay with his nose pressed into the damp soil and the leaves piled over his head, but a sense of calm and peace and hope replaced the sorrowful sobbing. And that was when he suddenly knew someone was standing on the trail in front of him. He didn't hear anything. He just knew he was there.

It's probably the owner of the dogs, looking for his escaped pack. How will I explain this? I'm not even sure I know what I'm doing.

Normal pushed himself up onto his knees and sat back on his feet. Damp leaves tumbled down his back

9. Psalm 147:6-8

and into his lap. Several remained in his hair and stuck to his shoulders. As he picked a wet leaf from his right ear, he chuckled awkwardly and said, "Sorry, I uh ..." but no one was there. Surprised, he stood and looked behind the trees on his right and left. No one.

As he brushed the leaves from inside his collar and out of his hair, a thought took his breath. He turned cautiously. No burning bush was behind him.[10] He breathed, a bit relieved but also a bit disappointed.

"Anyone there?" he called. No answer. The sun warmed his face. It was a bit lower in the sky, but not much. He looked at his watch. It had been an hour and seven minutes since he left his cabin. He was surprised. He thought it had been much longer.

Another unusual thought struck him as he walked back down the mountain trail. Entering the cabin, he went immediately into the bathroom. Cautiously, he peeked into the mirror. His face wasn't shining, but he did see a couple of leaves in his hair.[11]

Normal didn't know how he would explain to his family what had just happened. He wasn't sure he could. He wasn't sure he knew. Was his imagination running wild? Maybe. But he knew one thing; the Creator of the universe, his Savior who died on the cross, had heard his prayer and accepted his worship. That was real.

10. Exodus 3:2-4
11. Exodus 34:29

Chapter 6

THE SEARCH

Everything was different than when he began that morning. With a sense of approaching discovery, Normal returned to his worktable to continue examining his life.

Job

Normal liked the old Navy slogan, "It's not just a job. It's an adventure." He had not served in the Navy, but it described his attitude about his work. It was more than a job or even a career. It was an adventure he enjoyed. He was good at his work and was respected by his boss, his peers, and those who worked under his management. Every year he received commendations, bonuses, and was usually offered another promotion. Every year that is, except this one. He began writing.

> Is work hindering my satisfaction, or
> is dissatisfaction hindering my work? I am
> better at my job than many of my peers, but
> my productiveness has declined. Mr. Boss-
> mann tries to understand, but his patience is
> wearing thin. He deserves better work than
> I have given in the last few months.

Normal remembered an applicable passage and clipped it into his notes. It reminded him that his job was more than a career. It was a calling and a spiritual responsibility. His job actually mattered to God, and Jesus was his real boss.

> [5] Bondservants, be obedient to those who are
> your masters according to the flesh, with fear
> and trembling, in sincerity of heart, as to Christ;
> [6] not with eyeservice, as men-pleasers, but as
> bondservants of Christ, doing the will of God
> from the heart, [7] with goodwill doing service,
> as to the Lord, and not to men, [8] knowing that
> whatever good anyone does, he will receive the
> same from the Lord, whether he is a slave or
> free (Eph. 6:5-8).

Normal evaluated aspects of work: his relationship to those up and down the company ladder, and with his peers. Then he focused on the work itself. Normal discerned two problems with his job. First, his recent distraction had eroded his efficiency. Second, he now realized his failure to be a true friend to any of his work associates. After quite a bit of thought, he concluded:

My dissatisfaction hinders my work. My work isn't causing my dissatisfaction.

House

Normal wasn't sure why he listed his house. Shortly after he and Average married, they purchased their first home. It was a modest two-bedroom house on a small city lot, but it was a move up from their cramped garage apartment. His business education taught him the value of property ownership. He paid extra on the principal each month, steadily increasing equity and shrinking the mortgage. Just before Happy was born, they sold the little house and moved into a three-bedroom colonial. They repeated the scenario two more times. Three years ago the family moved into their dream home with a smaller mortgage than they had on their first home.

Normal bought a 5-acre lot and hired a contractor to build a customized home. Everyone in the family participated in the planning. Moody and Happy contributed ideas for the overall plan, and designed their personal suites. Average decorated and chose everything she wanted in the kitchen, dining room, and family room. She also decorated the master suite, two guestrooms with private baths, and helped the kids design a family/game room. Normal designed a study and "man cave" that he and Happy enjoyed. Now and then, the girls joined them for a game as well.

The house was finished almost on time and close to budget. Because of his great planning, and some "sweat equity," they moved into the house with a mortgage of less than 40% of the property's value. Normal looked forward to the family dream home being free and clear, five years and seven months after construction.

Normal enjoyed doing the maintenance on the house and property. The physical work contrasted well with his 40-50 hours a week at the office. It also gave him extra time with Happy, who always enjoyed working with Dad. *No way our house is the problem.* Normal wrote:

Thank you Father for a warm, comfortable, secure place to live.

Vehicles

This is silly. Average and I have the vehicles we want and the means to trade for others if we wish. Maybe I'm just going through a mid-life crisis.

Normal looked at "Vehicles" on the screen. The simple fact that he had written this heading discouraged him. It was a sign of desperation. *With all the blessings and prosperity I have, how could I be dissatisfied?* Yet Normal **was** dissatisfied. No matter how much he tried to convince himself it was ridiculous, it didn't change the fact. He continued.

Retirement

Normal realized he had reached the last page. Retirement? *Maybe this is it. Everyone worries about retirement. Is my answer here?* He began.

> <u>A place to live</u>: No. That is covered; we can stay in our house or sell it and move any place we wish. The sale will be 100% profit. No debts to pay off.
> <u>Retirement income</u>: My portfolio is healthy. Barring a financial collapse, my investment strategy will keep it growing. No one but God knows the future, but our investments should allow for a comfortable retirement and a helpful inheritance for children and grandchildren. Not to mention my company pension and lifetime health insurance.

Remembering a sermon from Pastor Goodman's "Living and Dying with Wisdom" series, "A good man leaves an inheritance for his children's children" (Prov. 13:22), Normal felt satisfied with his accomplishments. He understood the Lord's blessing on his life was the real reason he was in such great shape financially. He was as prepared for retirement as any man in his forties could be, and he was thankful.

> <u>Retirement health?</u> No one knows what health challenges the "golden years"

will bring. Average and I are doing all we can to stay healthy. Honestly I'm not worried. We live healthy, active lifestyles. We get annual physicals. Both of our families have longevity in our genes. Besides, we know our Lord will be with us, no matter what comes our way.

As far as I can tell, retirement holds no fears or sources of dissatisfaction.

* * * * *

Normal clicked the "page down" button. As expected, nothing happened. There were no more pages. "Wishful thinking," he said. "I planned my strategy, worked my plan, and came up empty. What now?"

Chapter 7

THE DISCOVERY

Normal decided to review his notes to see if anything new popped into his mind. He hungrily read each page until he was sure he had examined each area of his life. Aside from the faith, family, health, and friends sections, Normal was struck by the superficiality of his inquiries. They had to do with stuff—temporary stuff. He had no dissatisfaction about stuff, but the thought led to a question.

"What if I were the rich young ruler? If Jesus said to me (he did a Bible search to find the exact wording), 'You still lack one thing. Sell all that you have and distribute to the poor, and you will have treasure in heaven; and come, follow Me' (Luke 18:22), what would I do?"

Normal thought it over. He tried to be honest with himself and with God, as honest as one can be in a "what if" scenario. If I knew my stuff was causing my dissatisfaction, I'd put it all on sale tomorrow. Or give it away. Normal's months under the dissatisfaction cloud had one positive effect. It was clarifying the truly important things in his life—relationships. At the moment, his stuff seemed less than insignificant.

Normal remembered an idea in a Proverb, but since he had no idea where it was or the exact wording, he did a search in his Bible program. After several failed attempts, when he used wrong phrases, he finally found it. He read it several times, then turned the Proverb into a prayer.

> 7 Two things I request of You
> (Deprive me not before I die): [Lord, please grant these two requests, and if it's OK, I'd like to get them before I'm on my death bed.]
> 8 Remove falsehood and lies far from me; [Give me a clean and honest heart, mind, & character.]
> Give me neither poverty nor riches— [May I be satisfied in You, Lord.]
> Feed me with the food allotted to me; [I trust You.]
> 9 Lest I be full and deny You,
> And say, "Who is the LORD?" [Protect me from pride, arrogance, & self-righteousness.]
> Or lest I be poor and steal,
> And profane the name of my God (Prov. 30:7-9).

I trust You to give me enough to care for my
family, enough to be satisfied, but not enough to
be proud. I choose to be satisfied in You and not
in my stuff.

After the prayer, Normal continued his review.
None of the headings raised red flags in his mind, except one — "Friends." Reviewing the note page, he
was drawn to the statement, "But there is a friend who
sticks closer than a brother" (Prov. 18:24). When he
tried to move beyond it, he was drawn back to that one
sentence.

Something about the statement bothered and encouraged him at the same time. If it wasn't the cause of
his dissatisfaction, somehow it was related. The idea of
such a friend began to burn within him.

Normal sat staring at his notes, reading the Scripture passages over and over. Time passed. Propositions
gradually formed in his mind.

A true friend is someone who:

- Comforts,
- Protects in times of trouble, and
- Makes his friend a better man.

Before he knew it, Normal had been meditating
on the Scriptures, longing for a friend, praying for a
closer-than-a-brother friend for over two hours. A deep
hunger slowly replaced his dissatisfaction.

"That's it," Normal said aloud, as if explaining it to himself. "My dissatisfaction is unsatisfied hunger. I'm hungry for a true friend! I NEED A FRIEND WHO STICKS CLOSER THAN A BROTHER."

Normal suddenly realized tears were streaming down his face. And he was laughing. "Am I losing my mind?" he laughed. He wiped his face with his handkerchief. "Or am I finding it."

Normal felt as if he were emerging from a cave after several hours, suddenly aware of the world around him. He noticed it was dark outside and realized he hadn't eaten since his pre-dawn breakfast. It was 10:07 P.M. His unplanned day of prayer and fasting, self-examination and Scripture meditation left him feeling closer to the heavenly Father than he had been in many years. God's presence seemed to permeate the cabin. At the moment, his spiritual hunger was greater than his physical hunger, though the thought of food was reviving his appetite.

What was Normal to do now? Should he heat a can of something from the cabin pantry? *Is a can of baked beans a good way to break a fast?* He wasn't sure. Maybe he should go to bed and try to sleep. At that moment, he couldn't imagine being able to sleep.

Prayer was becoming Normal's default response to every question—the habit had developed over recent months. "What should I do, Father? Should I continue fasting, or should I heat a can of beans? Do you have more to tell me tomorrow, or is my mission here complete?"

Almost instantly a plan formed in his mind. Even though his family wasn't expecting him until tomorrow afternoon, Sunday, or even Monday, he would go home, get some sleep, and make Saturday morning breakfast for his family. He would conclude his fast with pancakes and sausage. He needed to tell them about his discovery. He would be home soon after midnight if he left right away.

Normal gathered his things, made sure the fire was out and the lights off, and headed for his truck. As he turned around in front of the cabin, the truck lights illuminated the brook. "As the deer pants for the water," he sang, "so my soul longs for a closer-than-a-brother friend."[1] He was even on key. *Father, help me find that friend.*

Just after midnight, Normal walked quietly up the stairs. His discovery had replaced despair with hope. His family was resting. He slipped under the covers beside Average. Though she wasn't awake, she patted the side of his head.

---

1. Martin Nystrom, "As The Deer," (Maranatha! Music, 1984); accessed Feb. 10, 2016, http://www.higherpraise.com.

Chapter 8

THE HUNGER

"I smell sausage," Happy said as he bounded into the kitchen, landing on a barstool. Mail was no longer stacked on the stools. "Hit me with a sausage, Dad. I'm open."

Normal didn't toss a patty across the kitchen. He delivered one to the bar on a plate. "And here's a fork," he said, but the patty was already in Happy's mouth.

"Didn't ethpect to theee you dis mornin'," Happy said, chewing and swallowing the sausage. "But I'm glad you're here, Dad. I love pancakes and sausage. Toss me another one."

"Save some for the girls. They'll be down soon."

Average entered the kitchen through the dining room. Her short brown hair was damp from her shower and brushed behind her ears. She had on a yellow t-shirt, jeans, and no shoes.

"How are my boys this morning?" Average asked.

"Wow!" Normal said, winking at Average. "I forgot how cute you are. Where've you been the last few months?" Normal smiled as he turned his attention back to the pancakes and sausages.

She slipped her arms around his waist and kissed the back of his shoulder. "Normy, I've been right here all the time," she said, snuggling up against his back. "Have you come back to me?"

"I'm great, Mom," Happy said, cheerfully, "but I need a little help. Dad's hoarding the sausage. Join the fight against teenage hunger in America: pass a couple more over here."

"Dad? You're home early," Moody moaned, leaning against the door jamb. She had on a bathrobe and her bed-head hair covered most of her face. "I knew it. Something's wrong. Is it bad? Did the cabin burn down?"

"No," Normal said, setting the platter of pancakes and sausages on the table in the breakfast nook. "Nothing's wrong. It could hardly be better. Breakfast is served. Moody, get the maple syrup out of the microwave on your way to the table. Happy, pour the orange juice, or milk if you want it."

Normal smiled and patted the back pocket of Average's jeans. "Sit down here little girl. Are you old enough to drink coffee?"

As they ate, Normal struggled to describe his day at the cabin. He wanted them to understand his search. He tried to describe his life-review that led to his search for the Bible's teaching about friends. He was hesitant to tell his mountaintop experience; it's hard to explain what you don't understand. He was afraid his family would think his anticipated mental breakdown had finally happened. To his surprise, when he tried to describe his mountaintop worship, his desire to get as low as possible, and the unseen presence, he was emotionally overwhelmed. He got choked up.

"I'm sorry," he said, wiping his eyes, a little embarrassed. He had never cried in front of his family.

Average held his left hand in both of hers, softly stroking the back of his hand. She knew something profound had happened to her husband.

Happy took another bite of sausage and shoveled two more pancakes onto his plate. "That's OK, Dad," he said. "Your water works just sprung a little leak. You'll probably feel better if you hand me the syrup. And the butter."

Moody sat up, pulled her sandy brown hair into a ponytail, and blinked. Her blue eyes were big. She was tuned in. Maybe there was a depth to his daughter he hadn't seen before.

Normal took a deep breath. "I think God is leading me on a journey and I don't exactly know where we're going, but I know I want to take you with me. That's why I'm trying to explain what I don't exactly understand. I realized this weekend that I've isolated myself from you. That was wrong and I'm sorry."

No one spoke for a long moment as Normal glanced from one to the other. He could tell they were supportive.

"I also know," Normal continued, "that finding my closer-than-a-brother friend is a big part of the journey. It's more than a need. I don't know how to describe it. It's a spiritual hunger."

Happy had reached his limit on serious conversation for a Saturday morning. Normal saw the twinkle in his eyes and knew an icebreaker was coming.

"Speaking of hunger," Happy said, "the pancakes were a step in the right direction. But warmin' some steaks on the grill tonight—that'll make you feel awesome, Dad. Who knows. Maybe that friend will smell them and drop by."

After Moody and Happy went upstairs to get ready for the day, Average said, "Honey, where do we go from here?"

"What do you mean?"

"I mean, what do we do next? You said I'm your best friend, but you need a different kind of friend. I understand that. It's a guy thing. But, you said your friendship with Typical is not what you're after. So, what's next? How will you find this friend?"

"I guess that's the next thing you can pray for."

"Ok," Average said, and bowed her head. She squeezed Normal's hand, then prayed, "Father, you know the deep hunger in Normal. You understand why it's there and what he needs. Dear Lord, please satisfy my husband's hunger. Help me to be the best wife I can be for him. In Jesus' name, Amen."

As Normal held Average's hands a moment longer, he knew he had never loved her more or felt a deeper intimacy with her. He wanted to look her in the eyes and express his feelings, but emotion was rising in his throat again. He smiled, stood and cleared his throat.

"I better get ready to take Happy to Karate."

"I love you too," Average said, and softly kissed his lips. She was standing on tiptoes with her arms around his neck. "Normy, we're on this journey together, wherever it takes us. You're not alone; don't forget it. But right now it's taking me to the dishwasher and you to the Dojo. See you at lunch."

Chapter 9

COMMUNICATING

After a quick shower, Normal drove Happy to his karate class. From the Dojo they headed for a father/son trip to the barber, then a stop for a 10-minute oil change (which took an hour and fifteen minutes), and on to the car wash. The morning included a divine appointment.

While waiting for the oil change, Normal and Happy eased into a natural conversation with a single mom, Desperate, who was struggling to corral her energetic, grumpy five year old. He was clutching some well-worn toys, but obviously they weren't entertaining him.

"What's your name?" Happy asked the boy.

"Needy."

"I'm Happy, and I'm glad to meet you. I see you have an awesome motorcycle, cowboy, and dinosaur."

"They're dumb," Needy said. He threw the dinosaur on the floor and kicked it under a chair.

"Are you kidding me?" Happy said enthusiastically. "I've seen these guys before." He picked up the Dinosaur and examined it. "Yeah, this is one of them. They're anything but dumb. Would you like me to tell you about the day they rescued me when my head was stuck to the wall by the bubble gum in my hair?"

Within moments, Needy was captivated as Happy wove together a silly story about his adventure with the cowboy, the dinosaur, and the motorcycle. Needy giggled as he and Happy moved the toys to coincide with the story.

Normal turned his attention to Desperate. She was obviously grateful for some adult conversation. Almost before he realized it, Normal had shared a brief testimony about how to trust Jesus and about the children's ministry at their church. Desperate was interested and promised to meet Normal and Average at church the next morning. Normal knew Average could introduce her to the Mom's Connection group. They would take her under their wing.

Needy smiled and waved the dinosaur at Happy as he left with his mom.

"See you tomorrow," Happy said. "Don't go to sleep with gum in your mouth."

At noon they met Average and Moody for a sandwich at the local diner. "I don't know how it happened," Normal explained as he told about their morning adventure. "I sure was proud of Happy. He made Needy's day. And talking to Desperate about Jesus seemed, well, ... natural."

Following lunch, Normal and Happy returned to the house for an afternoon of spring yard work. The ladies headed off on a shopping trip, promising to purchase some steaks to grill that evening.

The guys were putting away their tools when the ladies pulled into the garage. Moody was driving. Happy pretended to panic, but today, Moody didn't mind. She admitted that he was funny ... sometimes.

Happy and Normal helped unload the shopping bags. With the chores complete, they returned to the yard to toss a football for a while. And that was when Happy surprised Normal.

"Dad, I've been thinking about when you had your nose in the dirt and the leaves on your head."

Normal jumped to catch a high pass and said, "What do you think?"

"First I thought maybe you forgot to tell us about falling down the mountain and scrambling your brains. That was some weird stuff, Dad. But then I remembered youth group."

"At youth group Wednesday night, Pastor Funjoy taught us about the Commander of Lord's army who surprised Joshua.[2] General Joshua was doing recon at Jericho when this dude with a drawn sword in his hand

_____

2. See Joshua 5:13-15

shows up. Josh asks, 'Are you on our side, or theirs?' And the sword guy says, 'Neither one. I don't take sides, I take charge.'

"Pastor F. said it wasn't an angel or anybody else. It was Jesus, because the J-Man hits the dirt on his belly and face and worships Him. Angels don't accept worship; only God does.[3] Did you know that, Dad? Anyway, Joshua says, 'What do you want me to do Lord? I'm your servant.' Jesus tells the General, 'You're on holy ground. Take off your sandals.' Then He tells him how to march around the city till the walls fall down. You know the story."

"Hit me with a pass, Dad. I'm open."

Normal was standing holding the ball. He thought his mouth was probably hanging open. He was stunned to hear Happy's thoughts.

Happy caught the pass, spiked it, and did a chicken dance. "The crowd goes wild," he said, pretending to be a TV Sports commentator. "Happy, the world's greatest wide-receiver, has done it again! He has caught the winning touchdown in the Super Bowl for the 9th year in a row!"

He picked up the ball and threw it back. "Anyway, one of the guys asked Pastor F. if Jesus ever shows up with a strategy nowadays, cause he sure needs to know how to put the moves on the French exchange student in our class. She IS a babe."

---

3. See Revelation 22:8-9

"Pastor Funjoy says Jesus is with us all the time by the Holy Spirit inside believers, but sometimes we may be more aware of Him. We might feel He's right there with us, even though we can't see Him."

"Nothing like that's ever happened to me, but do you think you were more aware that Jesus is with you than ever before? Maybe it really was Jesus or the Holy Spirit. I don't really understand all the Trinity stuff."

He paused a moment, thinking. Then Normal saw the familiar twinkle in Happy's eyes. "Did you take off your hiking boots? And if you did, did any of the trees die?"

"Very funny," Normal laughed, "but I think you're on to something. Makes sense. Maybe that's exactly what happened. Let's go fire up the grill."

"Great idea, Dad. I always like a big steak after I win the Super Bowl."

* * * * *

Happy took a plate of grilled corn into the kitchen and Moody came out onto the deck. She slipped under Normal's arm and hugged him, laying her head on his shoulder. Normal thought, *My baby girl has become a woman. She's taller than her Mom.*

She hugged him a moment longer, then said, "I don't know what's happening to you Daddy. But I think it's all good. You seem a lot happier today. And you've started talking about Jesus in a new way. I don't know. It's just different.

Moody slipped from under Normal's arm and sat cross-legged on the deck. "You talk about Jesus as if you know Him. Like He's a real person."

"Don't you think Jesus is a real person?"

Moody was quiet while Normal flipped the steaks and adjusted the flames. Normal looked at her. She wasn't brooding, just thinking. It was a nice change.

"Yes," she said.

"Yes?"

"Yes, I believe Jesus is a real person. He's not an action hero. He's not a character in a comic book; He's real. I trust Him. But I don't have the kind of relationship with Him that you've talked about today." She paused, thinking. "How can I know Him like that?"

"That's a really good question," Normal said. "When you figure it out, let me know. Honestly, this is all new to me. Yesterday, I discovered I didn't know Him nearly as well as I thought I did. But I think that when I finally meet my new friend, he'll help me get to know Jesus a lot better."

Normal cut into a steak. "Done enough for you?"

"Too red for me. Let's not take chances. I want to watch a movie tonight, not spend the evening in the ER."

Happy had just returned with a platter for the steaks. "Come on Moody. That one's just right. Live a little. It'll be the tenderest taste your mouth has ever experienced. Have no fear of Moody Cow Disease."

Moody rolled her eyes and went inside. Sometimes he wasn't funny.

After a great meal they moved into the family room to watch their movie. Moody announced, "I picked the perfect movie for tonight." She held it up proudly before inserting it into the Blue-ray Player. They all laughed as the title came on the screen: "Eat, Pray, Love."

Normal knew it was coming, but caught Happy's eye before he spoke. It was just in time. His mouth was already open.

Normal shook his head. "Don't say it. Let it go. Don't spoil her moment."

Happy pressed his lips together, locked them, and threw away the key. After a moment his cheeks and eyes bulged and he made the sound of his head exploding. But he managed not to comment.

After the movie the family headed for bed, but Normal stayed in the family room. It had been a great day, and Normal wanted to end with personal Bible reading and prayer. When he opened his Bible, he didn't know where to read. He flipped through the pages, reading a verse here and another there.

Then his eyes landed on the words, "I [wisdom] love those who love me, and those who seek me diligently will find me."[4] It was the last part of the verse

---

4. Proverbs 8:17

that caught his attention. "Those who seek me diligently will find me." Normal began to pray, "Lord, I've been
seeking You and Your wisdom. I'm seeking diligently. I
need wisdom to find a closer than a brother friend. I'm
seeking as diligently as I know how. Please help me! In
Jesus' name I ask these things, Amen!"

Another week had come to an end. Normal headed upstairs for bed with the inner assurance that his
Heavenly Father had heard his prayer and the answer
was on the way.

Chapter 10

FRIEND DAY

As Normal awoke, "There is a friend who sticks closer than a brother," played on a visual loop in his mind. The sense of excitement and imminent discovery he enjoyed the previous day had fizzled in the night.

He was rested, but not satisfied. He had slept without waking even once; this had not happened in months. But Normal didn't think of that. He was focused on Proverbs 18:24. His hunger for a "true friend" was like a weight on his chest.

"Dear God, help me," he pleaded. "I need a friend ... a true friend. I'm not sure I understand what that means, but I know I need one. I need a friend who sticks closer than a brother, who is a comforting presence, a protector in trouble, and will help me know Jesus better. Please Lord. Please. Connect me to the right friend. I'm asking, ... no, I'm begging in Jesus' name."

Normal was oblivious to the clock—until Average stepped into the room.

"Better get moving," she said. "We'll be late. You do remember it's Sunday, don't you?"

Her words jolted him out of bed, into the shower, through the walk-in closet and changing room, and out the door. The sky was overcast and dark clouds were on the horizon. Sprinkles dotted the windshield.

The ride to church was like any other Sunday. Average and Happy carried on an animated conversation.

Moody checked her hair and make-up ... sighed ... texted ... checked Facebook ... sighed ... checked hair and make-up ... Instagrammed ... panicked.

"Oh no!"

"What's wrong?" Average asked.

"Go back home. Please!" Moody groaned. "I have to change my shoes. Jovial's wearing the same ones. She'll be all gushy when she sees mine; I can't stand it. It'll ruin Youth Bible Connection."

"OK baby girl," Normal said. "We'll find one before you go to college." He turned on the intermittent wipers. The rain was mixed with sleet.

Moody sighed. It was hopeless. Dad was zoned out again.

Normal, in fact, was wrapped up in his friend-focused prayer. The car almost drove itself along the familiar route and into their usual parking space.

Happy's exclamation, "Look! They're here!" jolted Normal into the moment.

Desperate and Needy were walking toward the side entrance with Hospitable and her two daughters. Desperate saw Normal and Happy. She smiled and waved. Obviously, Hospitable had taken them under her wing. Needy was showing the little red-haired girl his dinosaur and cowboy.

"Looks like they're in good hands," Average said. "I'll meet them later."

Normal smiled. And it wasn't his familiar "church smile" that said, "Yes, I'm still depressed. Don't ask." It was a genuine smile.

Happy fist bumped his Dad, kissed his Mom, and raced toward the youth building.

"Five dollars, please," Moody said, holding out her empty hand to Normal. "Glum and Temperamental texted from Dippin' Donuts. They're bringing me a Latte. I'm gonna need it. You can't imagine how awful this morning is going to be."

"Nice to have friends," Normal said, and plucked a bill from his money clip.

As they entered the side door, Normal felt a small beam of hope. He took Average's hand. "Maybe the Lord will speak to me during Sunday School or in the service."

"I hope so, Honey." She squeezed his hand and hugged his arm. "I'm praying this will be the day."

They greeted other smiling couples as they poured coffee, selected their donuts, and settled into their usual seats—third row, right back corner. As usual, class began with five minutes for prayer requests and prayer. As happened every two or three weeks, Mr. Didaskalos, their teacher, called on Jeremiah to pray. As usual, Jere's prayer was confident, brief, and to the point.

Everything was normal, average, routine. Nothing unusual. No surprises—until that astonishing moment.

Normal could hardly believe his ears. Mr. D. announced, "Today we're taking a break from our regular series. I thought it would be fun to talk about friendship."

Normal's mouth dropped open.

"What is a true friend? Anyone?"

Class members chimed in with various answers. "Once again, you've given great answers," Mr. D. said. "I love it. Nothing left for me to do, but remind you of a few chapters and verses and fill in a little detail. This is going to be good; let's get to it. This could be the day we finish early."

Several chuckled. Mr. Didaskalos was always enthusiastic. He often suggested finishing early was possible, but it hadn't happened yet.

"Open your Bibles to Proverbs 17:17. I think Solomon mentioned a part of this verse a moment ago. Norm, when everyone finds it, would you read Proverbs 17:17 for us?"

Average nudged Normal and pointed to the verse on her iPad.® "He asked you to read it," she whispered. "And don't forget to breathe."

"Uh, … sure," Normal managed to say. The lesson's subject still seemed too good to be true. "Verse 17 says, 'A friend loves at all times, and a brother is born for adversity.'"

After thanking Normal for reading, Mr. D. commented on the two phrases. He continued with several verses about the meaning and benefits of true friendship. They also discussed being a true friend.

As much as Normal knew he needed the entire lesson, his mind tuned out Mr. D's insights, the class discussion, and the other Scripture passages. Normal's attention was captivated by the phrase, "A friend loves at all times." He was aware of sitting in the class surrounded by people reading and discussing the Bible, but he wasn't a participant. He was carrying on an internal dialogue.

How can that be? How can a friend "love at all times?" I'm certainly not that kind of friend. I love a few people, but not "at all times." Some days I don't feel like loving. People don't deserve to be loved "at all times."

Normal thought of the love chapter. He opened his Bible to 1 Corinthians 13 to read the description of "love."

Wow! If love is all these attitudes and actions, I crash and burn on the first two in the list: "Love suffers long and is kind." How can anybody do that all the time?

No one ever loved ME "at all times." Even my parents got impatient with me. And who could blame them? I don't. I didn't deserve love "at all times."

And what about Average, especially the last few months? I've exhausted her longsuffering and kindness a few times. I don't blame her either. She's probably been more loving to me than I would've been if the circumstances were reversed.

Do I love Average at all times? How about Moody and Happy? Sometimes Moody's exasperating and Happy is exhausting. Is it even possible to love someone "at all times?"

Then he noticed 1 Corinthians 13:8, "Love never fails."

Maybe that's what a closer-than-a-brother friend does. He loves at all times because his love never fails.... How? Does such a person exist?

"Honey. Earth to Normal." Average was standing, nudging his shoulder. "Class is over. Let's go." He stood and slowly made his way out the door, down the hall and stairs, through the lobby, and into the worship center to their usual seats—halfway back, to the left of the pulpit. They greeted those who usually sat near them. They greeted Faithful and Devoted who always sat in front of them.

Throughout the music, prayer, Bible reading, and giving part of the worship service, Average prompted Normal when to stand and when to sit. He was there physically, but his mind seemed to be in a distant land.

Discouragement was engulfing Average again. Her high hopes from the previous day were dashed. Normal was even more oblivious than usual. Little did she realize, this was the dark before the dawn. Normal was on the verge of his life-transforming discovery; he was approaching the final curve of his journey.

"A friend loves at all times." I think I see the puzzle pieces, but how do they fit together?

"There is a friend who sticks closer than a brother." That's it. That's who's in the puzzle picture—my closer-than-a-brother friend who loves me at all times. But who is it?

Normal looked up suddenly. He was holding Average's hand. She was gently squeezing and tugging. He realized everyone else was standing, except, of course, for Mrs. Quickie, who sat in her wheelchair at the opposite end of the row. She smiled at Normal's awkward acknowledgement as he stood.

Pastor Chorister was introducing the next song, as he strummed his guitar and the keyboardist played in the background. ". . . written by Joseph Scriven, who definitely needed a friend's comfort. He prepared for an army career, but poor health foiled his plan. Soon afterward, in 1844, his fiancée drowned the day before their wedding. Heartbroken, he emigrated from Ireland to Ontario, Canada. There he taught school for a time and found a new love. They were to marry in 1855, but after a short illness, she died too. Then Scriven heard that his mother was sick back in Dublin. He couldn't go, but he wanted her to know the comfort he had found. So he wrote a poem for her. He never planned for anyone else to see it, but you know it well. You know it as his famous hymn, 'What a Friend We Have in Jesus.'[1] We all need His comfort today. Let's sing it together."

> What a friend we have in Jesus ...
> Can we find a friend so faithful
>   Who will all our sorrows share?
> Jesus knows our every weakness;
>   Take it to the Lord in prayer!
> Precious Savior, still our refuge ...
> In His arms he'll take and shield you ...

The words of the familiar hymn were sinking in. *Lord, I'm glad I can pray about anything anytime. Please, will You let me meet my friend today?*

The congregation transitioned into the melodic praise and prayer:

> This is the air I breathe, ...
> Your holy presence, living, in me ...
> And I, ... I'm desperate for You.
> And I, ... I'm lost without You....[2]

Normal's mind flashed back to the cabin and the pursued deer drinking from the brook. And then it flashed on the screen: "As the deer pants [longs] for the

---

1. Joseph Medlicott Scriven, "What a Friend We Have in Jesus," (Converse, 1868); accessed Feb. 10, 2016, http://www.hymnary.org.

2. Michael W. Smith, "Breathe," (Worship, 2001); accessed Feb. 10, 2016, http://www.azlyrics.com/lyrics/michael-wsmith/breathe.html.

water brooks, so pants [longs] my soul for You, O God"
(Ps. 42:1).

The congregation joined in the chorus.

As the deer panteth for the water
So my soul longeth after Thee.
You alone are my heart's desire
And I long to worship Thee.

Chorus
You alone are my strength, my shield,
To You alone may my spirit yield.
You alone are my heart's desire,
And I long to worship Thee.

You're my friend [Normal could hardly believe it. There
it was again.] and you are my brother
Even though You are a King.
I love You more than any other,
So much more than anything.[3]

The music and the harmonious voices swelled
around him.

Normal didn't sing. He stood, unblinking, holding Average's hand, staring at the screen. The pieces of
the puzzle were moving into place. His heart began to
pound. And ...

_____

3. Martin Nystrom, "As The Deer," (Maranatha! Music,
1984); accessed Feb. 10, 2016, http://www.higherpraise.com.

Average was tugging his hand.

Everyone else was seated. Pastor Goodman was kneeling beside the pulpit, "... and may the truths we've sung become vivid, powerful, transforming realities as You speak to us from Your Word. In Your name Lord Jesus' we ask it, Amen."

Later, Normal had no idea how the sermon was introduced, the pastor's text or outline, nor did he remember an illustration. But it didn't matter. The puzzle pieces had fallen into place when Pastor Goodman proclaimed triumphantly:

> There He stands in the rubble of our fallen world! He's with us.
>
> Do you see Him?
>
> Sin enslaves, but Jesus redeems and sets us free. He rescues wandering sheep and brings us home.
>
> Do you know Him?
>
> The religious leaders of His day meant no compliment when they called him "a friend of tax collectors and sinners!"[4] But I'm glad He is. That means I qualify for His friendship.
>
> He's our risen Lord, and He'll never abandon us. Friend, He'll never abandon you.
>
> Jesus is the friend who sticks closer than a brother!
>
> Is He your friend?

---

4. Matthew 11:19

It wasn't as if Normal had never heard those words. It was just that he had never HEARD. Before, they were churchianity, a religious cliché. Suddenly they were a comforting relationship and personal reality. *How did I miss it? It's so simple!* It was a new revelation he had known for years. *Jesus is MY best friend. He's MY closer-than-a-brother friend who loves at all times!*

In that moment, Normal's long journey ended as abruptly as it began. His hunger was filled. His heart was satisfied. His mind was clear. All the pieces clicked together. He knew his friend.

"Yes! That's it! I see Him!" Normal said aloud.

Average was shocked. Normal never spoke aloud in a service. The closest he ever came was a whispered, "Amen." But now he spoke as if answering Pastor Goodman's questions.

The pastor finished his sermon and offered an invitation. Normal didn't usually respond, but today was different. Normal stepped into the aisle and walked quickly to Pastor Goodman. Others followed and were welcomed by other counselors.

"Why did you come forward today, Normal? How can I pray for you?"

"Pastor, I found what I've been looking for. You've said it before, but I finally understand. Jesus is my best friend!"

He could say no more, but no more was needed. Pastor Goodman understood. He offered a brief prayer

and Normal returned to his seat. The invitation continued. Others responded. God was working in the service.

Normal embraced Average, held her close and
whispered into her ear. "This was the day God answered
our prayers. Everything will be different now. I found
Him! I found my friend."

Chapter 11

AFTERGLOW

Average and Normal stood to one side of the aisle chatting with Desperate. Needy and the little red haired girl were nearby. The girl was holding Needy's cowboy. Hospitable was getting her baby from the nursery; the moms planned to take the children to lunch.

Desperate had met a couple of potential friends at the Mom's Connection group. She volunteered her intention to visit the following Sunday. Normal introduced her to his friends who paused for a puzzled, second look at the new Norm. He hoped Desperate's day was turning out to be as spectacular as his own.

Typical slapped Normal on the shoulder. "How you doing, Buddy? Hangin' in there?"

"Top of the mountain, man," Normal said.

When Typical saw Normal's face, his astonishment was obvious. "Are you serious? What happened?"

"Something great. Can we meet for lunch on Wednesday? Lots to tell you. Lots."

* * * * *

The sky was clear as they exited the building. The sun was shinning and a hint of warmth was in the breeze. It had turned into a beautiful spring day.

Moody slid into the driver's seat of their SUV. "My turn to drive."

"Shotgun!" Happy shouted.

Normal opened the back door for Average.

As Moody started the engine, Happy said, "Couple of questions? And these are important, so listen up. Before we're out of the parking lot, I have to know. Moody, after the 'shoe trauma' at Youth Connection this morning, are you suicidal? I mean, that could push anybody over the edge. It's right up there with earthquakes, house fires, and the wrong color of lip-gloss."

Moody smiled and tenderly rubbed his shoulder and the back of his neck. "I'm fine, darling. So sweet of you to ask."

As she shifted the car into gear she added, "And don't bother with your seatbelt little brother. You won't need it."

"Ding, ding, ding. Good answer," Happy said, and buckled his seatbelt.

"And now for the real question." Happy looked back at Normal. "What gives, Dad? Where's the zombie that drove us to church?"

"Obliterated. I don't think we'll ever see him again. At least I sure hope not."

Average squeezed Normal's hand and smiled. "Let it be so, Jesus," she whispered.

"I'm driving across town to the Chinese Buffet," Moody said. "Let's hear the whole story."

"Good. It'll take a little time to explain it."

"Did you meet that new friend you were looking for?" Moody asked. "Was he in your Sunday school class?"

"Not really. Well … He was there, but that's not where I met Him."

"So, you found an old friend?" Happy said.

"You might say that."

"I know, I know," Happy said. "You got a dog— man's best friend."

Dad laughed. Moody sighed. Mom said, "Why don't we just let Dad explain."

"Today I realized Jesus is my best friend."

Almost in unison, Moody and Happy said, "I knew that!"

Moody continued, "Is that what all this has been about? Come on Dad. You and Mom have taught us that for … for … well, for as long as I can remember."

"Yeah," Happy said, but amazingly said nothing else. He was looking at his dad. There had to be more to Dad's transformation than this.

"Don't get me wrong. I've known it. Over the years, the friendship became a concept and a cliché in my head. It wasn't real in my heart. We sang about it at church and tried to teach you kids. But, somewhere along the way, I lost the reality. The saddest thing is, I didn't even realize what happened. I stepped into the trap of doing religious stuff rather than living a daily, growing relationship with Jesus."

"Several months back, as you know all too well, I knew something was desperately wrong. But I didn't know what. You know I became obsessed with my search for an answer. The longer it went the more depressed and discouraged I became. It controlled my life, and it probably ruined yours. You guys prayed for me and tried to understand, and I began a journey, searching for the answer."

"Friday, when I spent the day at the cabin, I realized I was hungry for a 'true friend.' And today my hunger was filled."

"What did it?" Average asked. "How did you find Him?"

"Remember, when Mr. Didaskalos asked me to read in class today?"

"Yes."

"You may have noticed that after I read I kind of went off into my own little world."

"Kind of!" Average laughed. "Until you suddenly looked up a Bible verse, I was considering calling 911. I thought you were in a coma."

"Sorry about that. I just couldn't get the first phrase of Proverbs 17:17 out of my mind: 'A friend loves at all times.' For some reason, the thought overwhelmed me."

Normal explained some of his thoughts and questions.

"Then we went into the worship service. The first thing I really heard was Pastor Chorister telling the story behind 'What a Friend We Have in Jesus.' I wondered why he was talking. He never does that. But then I thought he was telling the story just for me. 'That's the kind of friend I'm looking for,' I thought. 'I need a friend who will help me through disappointment, sorrow, and despair. I need a friend who is closer than a brother, who loves me at all times.'"

"It seemed like the pieces of a puzzle were spread on a table before me. Somehow I knew the puzzle was a picture of my friend, and the pieces, one by one, were finally moving into place. Pastor Goodman's sermon pulled it all together. Suddenly, it hit me.

- I have a friend who sticks closer than a brother.
- I have a friend who knows me, even better than the three of you.
- I have a friend who knows everything about me, but loves me anyway.
- I have a friend who knows every failure and sin of my entire life.

- I have a friend who knows my every thought before I have it, every word before I say it, every action before I do it. He even knows why I think it, say it, and do it. But He doesn't reject me. He doesn't abandon me.
- I have a friend who loves me all the time—completely, unconditionally, and perfectly.

"Like fog lifting and the sky clearing, I suddenly realized, *Jesus is MY best friend!* After all these months of searching, I found Him. And He was right there all the time."

As they arrived at the restaurant for Sunday lunch, Average knew her husband had changed. She didn't understand it all, but she knew the Lord had answered their prayers. Normal appeared to be a new man. She saw a peace in his eyes and a joy on his face that she had feared would never return. She prayed that, this time, it would last more than a day.

At the moment, Normal's excitement was infectious. New joy was springing up in her heart as well. Just during the drive from the church parking lot to the restaurant she observed a change in Moody's attitude. Even Happy seemed happier than usual. As they entered the buffet line she wondered, *"What now? Where will we go from here?"*

Chapter 12

ABUNDANT LIFE

In the weeks that followed, Normal awoke most mornings feeling refreshed. Each new day brought renewed hope. He enjoyed a previously unknown freshness in his walk with the Lord, with his family, and his church. Even his work was more productive.

Whether feeling on top of the world or under the weather, Normal's growing relationship with his faithful Friend gave him confidence in Jesus' mercy and compassion. It gave him hope. He was learning to live Lamentations 3:22-24.

[22] *Through* the LORD's mercies we are not consumed,
Because His compassions fail not.
[23] *They are* new every morning;
Great *is* Your faithfulness.

²⁴ "The LORD *is* my portion," says my soul,
"Therefore I hope in Him!"

He could hardly remember what it was like to be
dissatisfied, discouraged, and depressed. In some ways it
was like those first few weeks after he trusted Jesus for
the first time. Yet, it was different. The relationship was
just as exciting but it had a maturity that was lacking at
the beginning of his spiritual walk. The Bible knowledge he gained since believing was unchanged. Yet, the
old stories seemed new.

Early in his Christian walk, Normal had great passion for Jesus but little knowledge. Over the years his
knowledge increased, but his passion faded. His focus
had turned more and more on other distractions. Now,
for the first time in his life, his knowledge and passion
worked hand in hand. His knowledge produced wisdom. His passion motivated every area of his life.

*This must be what revival is all about. I've heard
about "revival." I've attended countless "revival services." I've heard numerous sermons on revival (most
from 2 Chron. 7:14). I've participated in cottage prayer
meetings for revival and discussion groups about revival.
But this must be it.*

*I feel I've been made alive again, I've returned to
Jesus, 'my first love.'¹ I'm no longer 'lukewarm.'² This
is great!*

---

1. Revelation 2:1-7
2. Revelation 3:14-21

Lord, thank You for being my best friend and for helping me to realize it. Thank You for reviving me, filling me, and drawing me into a closer relationship with You.

* * * * *

One night around the supper table, Normal shared his progress with his family. "And today, I realized how much I've been talking to Jesus. It's kind of like Moody and her boyfriend."

"Daaad!"

"I'm not saying that's a bad thing. I'm making a comparison."

"I don't know if you want to go there, Dad," Happy said. "Sometimes they don't do much talking. They just listen to each other breathe."

Moody rolled her eyes.

"What I'm saying is: just like you and Heartthrob can't get enough of talking to each other, that's how I feel about the Lord. I talk to Him off and on all day while I'm working. When I get a free moment, I open His Word so I can hear from Him."

"All day, Dad?" Happy asked. "What do you talk about?"

"Anything. Everything! I ask Him to help with my work. I ask for wisdom to solve problems. I talk to Him about good things going on and about problems we face. I talk about temptations (I know you think I'm old, but I'm not dead), and I talk about you guys. I ask the Lord to be with you and help you to know Jesus as your best friend. I thank Him for each of you and tell Him how proud I am of you. I turn my Bible reading into prayers for you and for Mom and me and your grandparents and aunts and uncles. I pray for Pastors Goodman and Chorister and Funjoy. I pray for our church and I pray for our business. I pray for anyone or anything that comes to mind while reading and praying the Bible. I believe the Holy Spirit guides me in what to pray and how to pray it.[3] When I read a command, I pray I'll obey it, and I pray you will too. When I read about a sin to avoid, ... you get the point."

"Yeah, OK. We get it. Basically, anything and everything," Happy said, holding up his hands in surrender. "I read my Bible and pray every morning when I first get up."

"Me too," added Moody, "and I'm lovin' it. We made a pledge at youth group: 'Truth before Texting. Father before Facebook. Insight before Instagram. Bible before Breakfast.' Some of the things H. T. and I talk about are the things we read and pray in the mornings."

"Right. I'm keepin' the pledge. I like it too. Pastor Funjoy told us the 'pray about anything and everything' line. But I'll be honest, Dad. I've pretty much run out of anything and everything in 2 or 3 minutes. God knows about all my stuff anyway. I don't need to bug Him all day long."

"That's OK, Happy," Average said. "Prayer isn't a timed project. That would make it boring. Nobody

---

3. Romans 8:26

wants that. I think the point your Dad is making is that prayer is a natural part of your relationship with Jesus when you know Jesus is real, He is with you, and He cares about everything that matters to you."

"Exactly!" said Normal. "Moody, when you hear or see or read something that's important to you or to Heartthrob, who do you want to tell?"

"Heartthrob, of course. That's why we call or text one another several times every evening. I need to tell Glum and Temperamental all the important stuff too, but I want to tell H. T. first."

"Do you time your conversations with H. T. to be sure you've talked the required amount of time for the day? Do you check the time so you'll know how soon you can quit talking?"

"Of course not. He's my special friend. And, yes, in spite of Mr. Sensitive's ridicule, sometimes we do just listen to each other breathe while we do homework and stuff. We like being together. I don't think about a time requirement. I think about my friend."

"Very good. You've just explained why we have the "phones off at 8:00 P.M." rule. Otherwise, you would talk and text till midnight. But you've also described prayer when Jesus is your best friend. Prayer isn't an obligation; it's a privilege. Like Mom said, it's a relationship."

Average said, "It just occurred to me. Jesus can be your best friend and my best friend all at the same time. Isn't that wonderful?"

"I never thought of that either. But you're right. That is awesome."

"Moody, Happy, just like your Dad, I have rediscovered that Jesus is my best friend. More than anything else, we want you to experience the same thing. It's good to have special friends like Glum and Temperamental and even Heartthrob, but Jesus really is your best friend. He will never disappoint you. He'll be with you, always."

Normal could not have said it better himself, so he said nothing. He could see his children were tuned in to what Average had said. *Lord, thank you for what You are doing in our home. It's a far better journey than I could have imagined. Thank You for being OUR best friend.*

After a minute or so of comfortable silence, Average said, "Wow, look at the time. I'm feeling extra generous tonight. Leave your phones on the kitchen bar. Dad will plug them in for you, and I'll do your dish-duty tonight. Be sure you're ready for school tomorrow, then head for bed."

"I love it when you're feeling generous," Normal said, and kissed Average on the lips. He jumped to his feet to grab the cell phone chargers. "I'll help with the dishes too."

"Whoa!" Happy said. "An impressionable minor's in the room. No PDA. My dinner won't be as good coming up as it was going down."

"Right you are," Normal said in a Yoda voice. "Ascend the stairs, you should. Close the door, you should."

"I'm not a 100% sure," Happy said thoughtfully, pausing on the third step, "but I believe that qualifies as the worst Yoda impression this century."

Normal took Average in his arms and said to Happy, "If see it you do not wish, run you must. Smooch your mother I must."

Moody grinned as she walked upstairs. Happy ran as if terrified by stormtroopers, and slammed his door.

"I didn't know it was possible," Normal said, looking into Average's eyes, "but I believe I love you more every day. Moody and Happy too."

"Our Best Friend really is transforming us," she said, returning his embrace. "But one thing hasn't changed. The kitchen still needs to be cleaned. You clear the table. I'll put away the leftovers and load the dishwasher. I'm still feeling generous."

Chapter 13

MENTORING

"Thanks, Pastor Goodman," Normal said, settling into a comfortable chair at the small, round conference table in the corner of the pastor's office. "I appreciate you taking the time to visit with me today." He took a sip and placed his coffee cup on the table.

"My pleasure, Normal. I've been looking forward to this visit. If my eyes don't deceive me, you have something good to tell me."

Normal could hardly contain the excitement bubbling up inside. "That's why I wanted to talk to you." He summarized his story since their last visit. He reviewed his journey from dissatisfaction to discovery, and his recent vibrant, growing relationship with his Best Friend.

"The change is obvious Normal. I noticed it beginning about two months ago. Am I right?"

"That's about right. But I'm curious, Pastor. How did you notice?"

"One reason I sit on the platform during the musical part of our worship service each Sunday morning is to survey my sheep. I think most people would be surprised if they knew how much can be seen from there. Anyway, I pray for specific needs the Lord brings to mind. You and your family occupied quite a few of those prayers in the past year. But in the last couple of months, there's been more thanksgiving than intercession. I knew your burden had lifted. It shows on your face, in your body language, and in the way you relate to others. You've been far more tuned in to my sermons, and you've started singing again."

"Pastor, you always say, 'What's on the inside, sooner or later, shows up on the outside.'"

"Yes, and it's contagious. In this case, that's a good thing. It's evident that Average, Moody, and Happy have a new excitement about Jesus."

"That's what worries me."

"Worries you? I'm afraid you lost me there, Norm."

"I'm glad about their excitement. Mine too. But recently I've had this gnawing thought in the back of my mind. What if my passion fizzles again? I didn't even notice it slipping away last time because it was so gradual."

Normal took a drink of coffee, crossed his legs, and examined his sock. He appeared uncertain about what he should say next. Pastor Goodman enjoyed his coffee and simply waited.

"Through the years my walk with the Lord has been a roller coaster ride. I rededicated my life at revival meetings and spiritual emphasis weekends. I promised to become a witness, but my F.A.I.T.H. training grew chicken feathers at work. I rededicated my life to becoming a prayer warrior, but I ran up the white flag before the battle started. I even signed up to fast and pray for a day, but I got hungry. I got really excited about Bible study the first time we attended the New England Bible Conference, but ... maybe you know what I mean."

Pastor Goodman nodded and smiled. "I'm familiar."

"Eventually, I grew indifferent. I didn't realize it at the time, but when new spiritual challenges or new opportunities for spiritual growth came along, I resisted. Maybe I was thinking, 'Been there. Done that. Not gonna get excited again. Too much effort to end up where I started.'"

Pastor Goodman and Normal both took a drink of coffee. Normal scanned the pictures on the wall and glanced over a few titles on the bookshelves. Normal wished the pastor would speak. He always seemed to know just what to say, and Normal thought this would be a great time for him to speak up. But he didn't. He was relaxed, looking at Normal. When Normal finally looked back at him, the pastor took another sip of coffee and said with an understanding smile, "So you resisted?"

"Yes. I embraced a bland, mediocre Christian life, but I didn't know it. I wasn't trying to stay indifferent. I was trying not to be disappointed. Now I'm wondering if I'm over-excited again, headed for another fizzle and failure. I don't want to end up deflated and defeated again."

Normal paused again as if he had suddenly explained something to himself. He shifted, a bit uncomfortable. He was much less confident than he had been when he arrived at Pastor Goodman's office.

"As I'm listening to myself, I realize I'm afraid I'll wake up tomorrow and all the excitement about my Best Friend will be gone. I'll disappoint my family. I'll disillusion the people I've been encouraging to trust Jesus Christ as their Savior, Redeemer, Lord, and Friend. Don't misunderstand Pastor. I don't doubt Jesus. I trust Him more than ever. I believe the Bible more than ever. I just don't trust myself."

The verbal explanation was a personal revelation. The confident hope that had dominated Normal's heart and mind since his "Friend day," deflated within like a balloon.

"OK," said Pastor Goodman. "Nothing you've said shocks me or even sounds strange. But I'm wondering, do you have a specific question?"

Normal carefully formulated his question before asking, "What can I do to stay passionate, to stay hungry but keep my hunger satisfied?"

"Normal, that is a great question! The fact that you asked it is a good sign."

Normal knew he had hit on something dear to Pastor Goodman's heart. It was apparent he had given the subject a lot of thought.

"Believe it or not, you've just described my early years of ministry. I would have been a ministry dropout if I had not found the answer to your question."

Renewed hope flickered to life within Normal. The balloon re-inflated a little.

"There are really two issues we need to discuss. First, we need to talk about 'feelings,' second, about 'filling.'"

"Pastor," Normal chuckled, "you even alliterate your conversations."

"Trying to help us remember," he said with a twinkle in his eye.

"OK. Got it. Feelings and filling."

"Norm, take a look at this illustration. Pastor Goodman had pulled a small paperback off of a shelf and opened it on the table in front of Normal. "An old fashioned, coal-powered steam train can help us understand this important truth."[1]

---

1. Based on The Train Diagram, *Handbook for Christian Maturity* written by Bill Bright. Copyright 1982, 2007 Campus Crusade for Christ Inc. All rights reserved. Used by permission.

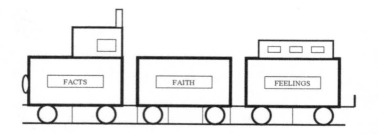

"Wow! Even your pictures are alliterated."

They both laughed.

"The 'Faith' coal tender represents your response to Jesus," Pastor Goodman said, pointing to the illustration. "The track is the path to continued growth in your relationship with Jesus. That's where you and I both want to travel."

"Right. And I guess that's where I've been derailing."

"Likely. But let's focus on present faith instead of past failures. Notice the engine and caboose. Which two of the three cars are necessary to keep the train running down the growth track?"

"Unless this is a trick question, the answer's obvious. The 'Fact' engine and the 'Faith' coal tender."

"Correct! Our Christian life is founded on biblical, eternal, God-revealed facts. But don't miss this. It's founded on facts, but fueled by your faith. Both are required for the train to function."

"I see that."

"You've already learned the fact: Jesus Christ, your Redeemer, Savior, and Lord is also your best Friend! Will that fact ever change?"

Normal thought for a moment. "During my months of searching, and maybe for years before that, it didn't seem to be true for me. So, I guess I better ask you. Does that fact ever change?"

"I'll answer your question with a question. What did you learn from Proverbs 18:24?"

"But there is a friend who sticks closer than a brother," Normal quoted.

"Is that a fact or a feeling?"

"Humm. If God stated it as a fact, it's a fact."

"So, Norm, which car were you trusting to take you down the track toward spiritual growth for all of those years? Fact or feeling?"

Normal felt a light had turned on. "I see what you mean, Pastor. My roller coaster Christian life was focused on the caboose instead of the engine. It's so simple. How'd I miss this? I was trusting *my* feeling instead of God's *facts*."

"Beautiful, Norm. I couldn't have said it better. The reality is, some days we feel Jesus' closeness and friendship. Those are great days. The little red caboose is with us, rolling happily down the track. But other days, the caboose is nowhere to be found. You may not know how or where or why it was disconnected, but it doesn't matter. You don't need a caboose to continue up the track, growing in grace. When the caboose is gone, your faith rests in the FACT: Jesus is still your Savior. He's still your Lord. He's still your best Friend. He does NOT change. He still loves you. Norm, I know you are studying Experiencing God by Henry Blackaby with your small group right now. You know Blackaby teaches us that your problems don't change the reality of the cross.[2] Your doubts and fears don't change it either. Feelings come and go but the Facts remain true for one reason: God is faithful. Does this make sense?"

"Absolutely! This is great stuff."

Normal was feeling excited again. "But you said there were two things. Wait. Don't tell me.... It was alliterated.... Oh yeah, 'feelings and filling.'"

"You're hitting on all cylinders Norm. I'm proud of you. The key to staying close to Jesus is simple. In fact, it is so simple many miss it. The Bible talks about it in several places. It uses various descriptions. In one place the Apostle Paul said, 'And be not drunk with wine ... but be filled with the Spirit.'"

"But Pastor, I haven't been drunk for years. In fact, I haven't had an alcoholic beverage since college."

"That's good, but you missed the point Normal. Paul is making a contrast and a comparison. The key is to be 'filled with the Spirit.'"

"OK. I'm not sure I understand the contrast and comparison, but tell me, how do I get filled?"

---

2. Henry T. Blackaby and Claude V. King, *Experiencing God: Knowing and Doing the Will of God.* (Nashville: LifeWay Press, 1990), 97-98.

"When a person is drunk, he or she is under the control of the substance that caused the intoxication?"

"Yeah. That's why the police call it, 'driving under the influence.'"

"Exactly! To be filled with the Spirit means to be under His influence, under His control. Another verse commands us to 'walk in the Spirit.' The idea is the same, just a different illustration. Moment by moment, step by step, we yield ourselves to our Lord Jesus. Our 'walk' is our consistent lifestyle. As we walk in the Spirit, He consistently controls us. His control, His influence, His filling is the consistent pattern—our consistent lifestyle. When He is in control, He leads us into a closer friendship with Jesus. People around us are impacted because the closer we walk with Jesus, the deeper our friendship grows and the more we act like Him."

Normal was quiet for a few moments as he stared at the train illustration. "Feelings and filling. I see it now. Don't be controlled by my feelings; be controlled by the Holy Spirit. Faith in God's facts will fuel my engine, the Spirit will keep me on track, and I'll move toward growing in my relationship with Jesus—with or without feelings."

"Again, couldn't have said it better myself, Normal. Let's pray before you go."

After Pastor Goodman's prayer, Normal made a bold request. "Pastor, I know you're busy and have a lot of other sheep in your flock, but I suspect there are a few other simple things I've missed. Would you be willing to meet with me once a month? I want to stay on track."

Pastor Goodman stood and shook Normal's hand. "I'd be honored to, Normal, but there are two require- ments. When I give you homework, we can't meet again until you have done it."

"No problem! I'd love it," Normal said as he slipped on his jacket.

The pastor continued as they stepped toward the office door. "Second, if I mentor you, you must be will- ing to mentor another man—someone who could use the same help you are receiving. It's the Second Timo- thy 2:2 principle. "And the things that you have heard from me ... commit these to faithful men who will be able to teach others also."

"That's a bigger challenge, but if you'll help me find the right man, I'll try."

Pastor Goodman grinned and said, "Was it Charles Spurgeon or Winston Churchill? Maybe it was Mark Twain. Anyway, someone said, 'There is no try. There is only do or not do.'"

"That was Yoda in one of the Star Wars movies," Normal said. They both laughed.

"Very good Normal. You're a natural. Mentoring is telling someone else what you know. Be filled, be willing, and God will lead you to the right person at the right time. Just like he brought you here today."

They agreed on a time to meet the following week for Normal's first homework assignment.

Chapter 14

SHARING

"And the fringe benefits are great too!"

Average, Moody, and Happy could hardly believe their eyes. Normal was behind the pulpit sharing his "personal revival" testimony. It was Sunday morning, six months after his "Friend day," and more than a year since Normal's Journey began. He and Pastor Goodman had been meeting periodically for four months.

Their church's worship-center was comfortably full, even though it was the second service of the morning. The recently added service was one of several indications that God was actively working in their church body, as well as in Normal and his family.

After a couple of humorous comments, Normal had expressed his excitement about God's fresh work in their church. He expressed gratitude for his Sunday school teacher and class, he celebrated Pastor Funjoy's ministry to their teens, and he thanked Pastor Goodman for his preaching and mentoring ministry.

Average smiled and kept her eyes focused on Normal's face. If he glanced her way, she wanted him to see her support and encouragement. Silently she prayed, *"Lord, fill my husband with Your Spirit. Use his testimony to draw other believers into a growing friendship with You."*

Moody couldn't believe her eyes or ears. On the drive to church that morning, her dad had been nervous and unsure of himself.

"If you're so nervous," she said, "why not tell the pastor you changed your mind?"

"Can't. It's my homework," he said, but that made no sense.

All during the Sunday school hour, Moody hoped her Dad had come to his senses. She hoped he explained to whoever was in charge of the service that he had made a mistake; he couldn't speak in front of the whole church.

But what she feared, happened. Pastor Chorister didn't skip the testimony slot in the service schedule. He introduced her dad, and her dad actually got up and walked to the pulpit. She was so embarrassed. No, mortified was a better description.

Don't Dad. Why are you going up there? You'll stammer and cough and ramble. You'll humiliate me. And My friends..., O, I don't even want to think about it. Daaad! Why are you doing this to me? You're an accountant, not a preacher…. This is so awful. She covered her eyes in shame. She couldn't look at her friends.

But then she realized … he wasn't embarrassing her. He was funny and interesting and was saying just the right things in just the right way. Her friends weren't sighing and rolling their eyes. They weren't making fun of her, pretending to sympathize and feel sorry for her. Even Glum and Temperamental were listening. In fact, they appeared to be hanging on his every word!

Moody knew he had changed, but this was unbelievable. He talked about her mom and her brother and now he was talking about her—how much he loved her and how proud he was of her, and about her going to Northeastern Baptist College in the fall, and about how Jesus was transforming their family, and she knew it was all true, and Temperamental whispered, "Wow!" and then she looked a Moody with a tear, an actual tear in her eye and said, "Your dad …", and squeezed Moody's hand, … and she was OK and everything was better than just alright.

Moody wasn't embarrassed any more. Her dad had something important to say, and people were interested. To her amazement, they were quite moved. God was actually using her dad! Moody was a little ashamed for doubting him instead of praying for him. *I guess this really isn't all about me.*

But most of all, she was proud of her dad. She knew it was because he had discovered his Best Friend. And now it was becoming clear. It was all about Him.

Happy was ... well ... happy. Excitement beamed from his face as he listened to his dad's brief description of his journey from confusion, depression and desperation, to satisfaction.

Normal continued.

"The greatest thing about my new walk is knowing Jesus better than ever. Growing in friendship with the Lord is transforming every part of my life. However, when I reflect on the fringe benefits, I'm overwhelmed by God's blessings. Let me mention just a few."

"First, I now have a closer relationship with my wife. It's amazing. The closer I get to Jesus, the more I enjoy my friendship with Him, the closer I am to Average. Some days I think, 'I could never love this woman more.' But then a few days later, I realize I do. Our relationship has grown deeper as we have learned to pray together. I'm sorry to admit, we never did that before, unless we were in a crisis. Now we pray together almost every day. And you know, it isn't a chore. Some days we only pray a couple of minutes. Other days it's 10 or 15 minutes or more. We aren't keeping a time log. We aren't fulfilling an obligation. We are two great friends, together, talking to our Best Friend."

"Second, there is the relationship with the kids. Moody and Happy are great. I'm so thankful for them. I've always enjoyed being their dad, but our relationship is better than I ever imagined. I want them to know Jesus as their best friend as well."

"Our son, Happy, is my buddy. Those of you who know him know why I say he's my bubbly buddy." He went on to tell how they were learning to talk man-to-man, heart-to-heart, and he told how he and Happy had become a witnessing team. "I don't know what it is," he said, "but I know God has something special planned for our son."

Then he talked about the fringe benefit of being Moody's dad. He told how she was going away to college, how proud he was of her, and how he hoped some of the other seniors from their youth group would go with her to Northeastern Baptist.

"But most important," he said, with a pause to control his emotions, "God has shown me that if I'm to have a Godly son-in-law some day, a son-in-law who knows Jesus as his Best Friend, I must set the standard now. I can show her how a Godly man loves his wife and children. And I hope and pray that some day she will say, 'Daddy, I'm getting married today, but I want you to know I didn't lower the standard. I waited for God to bring me a husband just like you.' I'm not that man yet, but I'm thankful I'm finally on the right track."

Average noticed some ladies brushed a tear from their cheeks, and Moody saw the same among her friends. More than a few men suddenly needed to clear their throats and examine the lights and the condition of the ceiling.

"We've begun a new thing in our home," Normal said. "We're reading the Bible and praying together for the first time. We do it just after supper. We bought a *One Year Bible*, and that's our reading plan. In case you haven't seen one, it has an Old Testament reading, a reading from Proverbs, a Psalm, and a short New Testament passage for every day of the year. It takes 15 minutes, more or less, but it's amazing. We thought we knew our Bibles, but we're discovering stories we didn't know were there. We're also learning that some things we thought were in the Bible, aren't. When we read the whole story, instead of a verse or two, we get a new perspective. Our teenagers are into it as well. Bible reading has led us into some surprising family discussions. I can't explain it, but prayer and simply reading the Bible have brought a fresh harmony into our home. That was a surprising fringe benefit. Maybe it would do the same for you."

"And there are fringe benefits at work. Wow! At least once a week the Lord gives me open doors with my co-workers. I've been able to share the Gospel with over 20 people now, and some have trusted Jesus as their Savior. In fact, some are here today, including our firm's owner, Mr. Bossmann. Before, I hardly ever shared my faith. I don't know, maybe that was a good thing. Why would anyone have wanted a Christian life like mine? I certainly didn't. But now that Jesus is my Best Friend, people almost beg me to share with them. Spiritual conversations just seem natural. It's easy to talk to friends about your Best Friend."

"I could say a lot more, but I better sit down. My 5 minutes were up a couple of minutes ago and I see Pastor Goodman is fired up. I can't wait to hear what he has to say. I'll end with the best news I can share. If you've trusted Jesus, run to Him. Get to know Him. He'll welcome you, because He's *Your* Best Friend!"

As Normal sat down beside Average, a holy hush was over the congregation. Several were bowing their heads in prayer, until Happy, who was sitting with his buds, half way back on the other side of the worship center, jumped to his feet, pumped his fist and yelled, "You go, Dad!" People laughed, and first a few, then several, then everyone, stood and applauded.

Pastor Chorister, who was now at the pulpit, said, "As long as we're standing, let's sing a verse of, 'What A Friend We Have in Jesus,' then transition into the chorus, 'I'm so glad, I'm a part of the family of God."

After the service, several people stopped Normal to thank him for the testimony. Typical was one of them. He said, "We've been friends a long time, but I'd like to get to know the new Normal. I think I'm gonna' like him. By the way, ..." Typical hesitated and seemed a little embarrassed, "this mentoring thing you mentioned. I, uh, ... think that's something I need. Would you be willing to mentor me?"

"Are you serious?"

"As serious as I would be about outrunning YOU, if a mad grizzly bear was chasing us."

"Then I'd be honored. But I have two requirements ..."

Part 2

PRINCIPLES
and
APPLICATIONS

Chapter 15

PERSONAL REVIVAL

Normal embarked on a journey from dissatisfaction to personal revival. In Part 2 we will revisit various aspects of Normal's Journey, note principles, and make applications for *our journey to personal revival*.

First, I'll define two key terms: *Revival* and *Spiritual Awakening*. Though some see them as synonymous terms, I view them differently.

I understand *Spiritual Awakening* to be God's movement in a region, state, or nation whereby a large number of non-believers are awakened to their sinful condition, realize their inability to save themselves, and turn to Jesus Christ in repentance and faith for salvation. In a spiritual awakening a large group of people are saved in a short time period.

Revival, in contrast, is God's work of renewing and refreshing spiritual life among genuine believers who have grown lukewarm, cold, and/or apathetic in their relationship with the Lord. Revival is a large number of saved people getting right with God in a short period of time. They turn from sin and indifference, to a renewed, refreshed, revived relationship with Jesus Christ.

Revival and spiritual awakening are both distinct works of God. Yet, the two interact with one another. God's people impact the lost. God uses His revived people in the process of spiritual awakening.

Jesus called Peter and Andrew. "Follow Me," He said, "and I will make you fishers of men" (Matt. 4:19). Believers who "follow" their Lord closely, lead others to faith in Him; revived believers impact the lost. God actively works through His children in both *Revival* and *Spiritual Awakening*.

Prior to revival, the Holy Spirit stirs up a holy dissatisfaction within a believer. He convicts the believer of his or her lukewarm, cold, apathetic relationship with God. The believer confesses his or her sin and is cleansed. The Holy Spirit then revives, renews, and refreshes the believer's relationship with Jesus Christ. He leads and empowers the revived believer to witness to unbelievers. The witness' transformed life and attitudes are evident, making the verbal witness credible.

In addition, the Spirit convicts the lost of sin, righteousness, and judgment to come (John 16:8-11). The Holy Spirit opens the door for the believer to share the gospel, and for the unbeliever to hear the gospel. He opens the unbeliever's eyes to understand the Word, so that he or she can respond in repentance and faith. "So then faith *comes* by hearing, and hearing by the word of God" (Rom. 10:17).

Revival and *Spiritual Awakening* are clearly the work of God. However, my emphasis here is that when God revives His children, He then uses them in the process of bringing spiritual awakening into the lives of lost men and women, boys and girls.

Usually when we refer to revival or a spiritual awakening we are referring to a large movement of God across a region, state, or nation. Such a movement is desperately needed today. Indeed, in my judgment, unless a genuine revival and spiritual awakening sweeps our nation, we may not survive as a free nation with religious "liberty for all" much longer. Further, I'm convinced a "large revival" most often starts with the "personal revival" of a few believers in various places.

As a few individuals experience personal revival, they become infectious to others in their immediate sphere of influence. The revival may spread through their churches, to other churches across a region. It can impact a state and even and entire nation. If God's people are truly revived, they become "fishers of men." This is the pathway to another Great Awakening.

What part will you play in reviving your church, region, or nation? You cannot respond to God for other people. You cannot revive other people's hearts. You can, however, prepare yourself for personal revival. You can have a clean heart[1] and a fresh, renewed relationship with Jesus Christ.

The following pages present key principles that can help you begin your journey toward personal revival. Of course, as the old time preachers said, "Before you can be revived, you must be vived!"[2] In other words, the principles described below assume you have 100% certainty that you are spiritually alive and you have assurance of a home in Heaven. You are secure in your personal, saving relationship with Jesus Christ. If not, please turn to the Appendix and read, "YOU CAN KNOW FOR CERTAIN, HEAVEN IS YOUR HOME."

If, however, you are certain you have eternal life, please read the following pages with an open mind. Each of the following short chapters will introduce principles from Normal's Journey that can help you proceed on your journey to personal revival. An application section concludes each chapter. The author's prayer is that the Lord will use these pages to guide you toward personal revival.

----

1. If we confess our sins, He is faithful and just to forgive us *our* sins and to cleanse us from all unrighteousness" (1 John 1:9). "Create in me a clean heart, O God, and renew a steadfast spirit within me.... Restore to me the joy of Your salvation, and uphold me by Your generous Spirit. Then I will teach transgressors Your ways, and sinners shall be converted to You" (Ps. 51:10, 12-13).

2. Heard numerous times from various preachers during childhood. Original source unknown.

APPLICATION

1. Confess your sin and trust Jesus Christ to cleanse you of all unrighteousness.
2. In Jesus name, ask God to give you a hunger for a renewed relationship with Jesus Christ.
3. Ask Him to help you understand His pathway to your personal revival.

Chapter 16

CONTENTMENT

In the most familiar Psalm, King David declared, "The LORD is my Shepherd, I shall not want."[1] Notice the cause and effect. The first phrase, "The LORD is my Shepherd," is the cause; the second, "I shall not want," is the effect—the thrilling consequence. If "the Lord" is your "Shepherd," every true need in your life will be met. That's not a health and wealth fantasy. It's what shepherds do for their sheep.

But even better, if "the Lord" is your "Shepherd," every longing will be satisfied. "I shall not want" is an astonishing confession. Today, you can go from clamoring for more to contentment with what you have.

Which is better: having everything you want delivered to your door, or being content with everything

---

1. Psalm 23:1

you have? Which option will satisfy you next week, next month, and next year?

Jesus said, "I am the good shepherd. The good shepherd gives His life for the sheep.... I am the good shepherd; and I know My *sheep*, and am known by My own" (John 10:11, 14). Because the good shepherd knows you and you know Him, you can "be content with what you have, for He has said, 'I will never leave you nor forsake you'" (Hebrews 13:5).

Believers can be content, and that includes you. Yet, many fail. Like Normal, they have a strong sense of dissatisfaction. Some try to ignore it, while others seek satisfaction through various means: professions, possessions, power, or popularity. Still others try religion, rules, and rituals. But none of these produce satisfaction.

Normal tried to overcome dissatisfaction with professional success and possessions. He advanced in his career and enjoyed the benefits. His self-esteem and bank account grew with each promotion. He built a dream house and bought a mountain cabin. He had a new truck and boat and snowmobile. When it came to big-boy toys and tools, Normal was a salesman's dream. He enjoyed his stuff and shared it freely, but the fix was always temporary. A new model always came out. A new season always arrived. A new distraction was always available.

It wasn't that Normal's lifestyle was immoral. Far from it. He was a moral example, a model employee, and an ideal neighbor. He was a family man (a wife and two children that made awesome family portraits) and man of faith. Normal wasn't a phony. His faith was real, but stagnant. He was a regular attender and active participant in his church, but he had drifted into indifference. Tragically, he didn't even know it.

Normal lived the "American dream," but it didn't fill the void. Dissatisfaction always lurked in the shadows. Finally it caught him, invading his safe-haven in the middle of the night. He awoke knowing something was seriously wrong. Once he acknowledged its existence and began searching for the problem, his dissatisfaction grew. Providentially, it propelled him in the right direction.

Whenever dissatisfaction reveals itself in your life, consider it an invitation to a closer relationship with Jesus. The answer to dissatisfaction is always Jesus. No matter how big or small the feeling, every believer can turn to Jesus Christ for contentment. Only a genuine, vibrant, growing relationship with Jesus produces true contentment and satisfaction. But when you find it, you can exult with David:

The LORD is my Shepherd,
I shall not want.

APPLICATION

1. Set aside some quiet time to ask yourself, "Is the LORD really my Shepherd?" If you are unsure of the answer, please turn to the Appendix and read, "YOU CAN KNOW FOR CERTAIN, HEAVEN IS YOUR HOME."

2. If the LORD is your Shepherd, take some time to honestly evaluate your life. Is dissatisfaction seeping in? Are you content? If not, maybe the Holy Spirit has placed dissatisfaction within your heart to draw you into a closer relationship with Jesus.

3. Are you trying to alleviate your dissatisfaction through some means other than Jesus? If so, confess this to Him. Ask Jesus to forgive you. Ask Him to help you find true satisfaction in your relationship with Him.

4. Ask the Lord to help you recognize dissatisfaction quickly and turn to Him immediately.

Chapter 17

CYCLE OF DESPAIR

Many believers are dissatisfied. Few understand the source of dissatisfaction. Ironically, some believers trap themselves in dissatisfaction with pseudo-spirituality. They know they should be content. They imagine that most others in their Christian circle are content. They don't want to acknowledge dissatisfaction for fear that God will be angry and their fellow believers will think them unspiritual.

Ignoring the problem never solves the problem. It usually makes it worse. Dissatisfaction can produce guilt. The guilt can lead to more dissatisfaction and more guilt. Guilt-induced dissatisfaction leads to depression and ultimately to despair. Believers can trap themselves in a vicious cycle. Examine the diagram below. Is it an illustration of your life?

Normal was in the despair cycle, but he couldn't find the exit ramp. He knew something had to be done; it was infecting every area of his life. Everyone around him realized something was wrong. Many offered advice, and Normal tried to follow most of it. Yet, no matter where he turned, his dissatisfaction grew. Every support system that Normal had built began to crumble under its own weight.

Call

In his despair, Normal's genuine faith was revealed. He turned to God for help. No longer did he have a ritual morning devotional. He desperately sought God. He prayed and searched the Scriptures. He knew that unless God answered, there was no answer. He shared his anxiety with his family and recruited them to pray for him.

Seek

Without realizing it, Normal switched onto the right track. He followed God's promise to His despairing children in Babylonian captivity: "Then you will call upon Me and go and pray to Me, and I will listen to you. And you will seek Me and find Me, when you search for Me with all your heart" (Jer. 29:12-13).

Normal headed to his mountain cabin for a day of intense seeking. He was alone with God, and God was faithful to His promise. That day, with no other distractions, Normal realized the missing piece in his life could not be purchased. He was missing a friend, a friend who sticks closer than a brother.

Silence

Our society does not value quiet, alone time. Everywhere we go we are bombarded with noise and screens, and we like it that way. Instead of being a useful tool, constant digital contact can become an ultimate distraction, and even an addiction. True satisfaction requires serious seeking, and serious seeking requires silence. The Bible says, "Be still and know that I am God" (Ps. 46:10). Being still is essential to seeking satisfaction.

APPLICATION

1. Schedule a daily quiet time for reading your Bible and for prayer.
2. Schedule an extended time to spend in silence before the Lord each month.
3. Have a single, simple goal: getting to know Him better.
4. Plan an entire day to be alone with God and truly seek Him, if possible, at least once a quarter. Trust that "those who seek Him diligently will find Him" (Prov. 8:17).

Chapter 18

FRIEND & FRIENDS

After a quiet day of serious seeking and life-examination, Normal discovered the source of his dissatisfaction. It was in the "Friends" file of his electronic journal. Initially, this was a mystery. He had many friends. His wife was his best friend on earth. He even had a hunting and fishing buddy. Yet, he was missing out on some mysterious area of friendship.

Normal looked for the answer in the right place. He invested a couple of hours in reviewing the "friend," "friends," "friendly," and "friendship" verses in the Bible. Meditating on and praying through specifically applicable verses led Normal to the next stage of his journey. He discovered he was hungry for a "true friend."

When Normal discovered that Jesus was his best friend, the true friend, the reality did not isolate him from other people. Instead, it connected him to others.

This is an important point. The principle, Jesus Christ is your true friend, does not mean you no longer need other people in your life. Jesus' friendship does not isolate you; it integrates you into other people's lives.

It's amazing, almost shocking, how many struggle with "friendship." Most Christians say, "Jesus is my friend," whether or not they understand what that means. Most believers have meaningful friendships with their spouse, their children, their parents, and within their local church. However, many lack a "true friend." Someone is missing from their lives.

Friendship Need

I've observed at least three futile attempts to deal with the friendship need.

Ignore

First, some do their best to ignore the feeling. As a result, they unconsciously avoid relationships. They tend to deal with people on a shallow, surface level. Other say, "He's a nice guy, but hard to get to know. He plays his cards close to his chest. You can never really know where you stand with him."

If you pride yourself on being mysterious, a loner, hard to get to know, at best you are avoiding relationships. At worst, you are sabotaging your relationships with your spouse, your children, with fellow believers, with work associates, and with God.

God made you in His image.[1] He is a relational God. He made you for relationships with other people and with Him. Ignoring your friendship need will consign you to a permanent emptiness in your heart.

Talk

Second, some talk about their search for a friend—frequently. It may be a weekly prayer request in their Sunday school classes or small groups. Unfortunately, such people tend to become self-obsessed and needy. As such, in their obsessive search for friendship, they drive potential friends away.

The person who has friends must be friendly.[2] That is, be friendly, not needy. The question is not, "Who will be my friend?" but "To whom can I be a friend?"

Church Hopping

Third, other believers spend a lifetime hopping from one church to another looking for friendship. For obvious reasons, most are disappointed. How could one build relationships if they abandon the project every time a difficulty surfaces?

Personal relationships without difficulties do not exist because no perfect people exist. True friends love through good times and bad. Again, Proverbs states, "A friend loves at all times" (Prov. 17:17). A friend doesn't bail out when the going gets tough. Likewise, finding a friend requires hanging in there, being willing to work through problems rather than run from problems.

---

1. Genesis 1:26-27
2. Proverbs 18:24

In all three cases, the problem is a sinful self-focus. The first person is self-sufficient, saying, "I don't need a friend." The second is self-obsessed, asking, "What's wrong with everyone else? Why won't they be my friends?" The third is self-protective, saying, "I'll never let anyone hurt me again."

After Normal discovered his "friend need," he refused to give up until he found his true friend. His true friend then reconnected him with his family, and integrated his life into many other lives—Desperate and Needy were an example.

I'm convinced Jesus Christ wants you to know His friendship more than you hunger to know it. So, don't give up. Don't abandon the search. You can discover the exciting reality: "Jesus is your best friend." He will then connect you with others.

APPLICATION

1. Are you hungry for a "true friend"?
2. What are you doing to seek "true friendship"?
3. How would you describe your friendship with Jesus?
4. Has your friendship with Jesus connected you with other people?

Chapter 19

FIRST LOVE

Do you know anyone who loves "at all times?"

Normal could hardly believe his eyes as he read to his Sunday school class, "A friend loves at all times" (Prov. 17:17). No doubt he had read the verse before. Yet this time, every word seemed to jump off the page. They captivated his heart.

Normal loved his wife and children. He could say, honestly, that he loved others outside their immediate family circle. But when he reviewed the "love chapter," he was acutely aware that he failed to love at all times. He also realized that no one, including Average and his parents, had ever loved him "at all times."

No mere mortal truly loves all the time. A brief review of 1 Corinthians 13 confirms the veracity of the statement.

Love suffers long *and* is kind; love does not envy; love does not parade itself, is not puffed up; does not behave rudely, does not seek its own, is not provoked, thinks no evil; does not rejoice in iniquity, but rejoices in the truth; bears all things, believes all things, hopes all things, endures all things. Love never fails (1 Cor. 13:4-8a).

Love, you will notice, is more than sentimental words. It is more than emotions or feelings. Emotions change and feelings fluctuate, but "love never fails."

Have you heard it said, "You can't tell a heart who to love"?

The Bible responds, "Of course you can." Love is not the servant of feelings; feelings are the servants of love. Love can function with or without feelings because love is a choice. Love is demonstrated in continuous, selfless attitudes and actions. One can choose to love, whether or not one feels loving.

Who can live up to that standard—all the time? Even the most loving falls short.

When Normal came to this realization, he was discouraged. He questioned whether or not a true friend even existed. Fortunately, he didn't abandon his search; he was closer than ever to his hunger being satisfied. Only one step remained—identifying his closer than a brother friend.

Normal met his true friend the moment Pastor Goodman said, "Jesus is the friend that sticks closer than a brother." With that realization, all the pieces fell into place. The puzzle picture was complete. Normal's search was finished.

The friend had been there all the time. When Normal shared it with the family, his children were shocked. They had heard it many times; it wasn't new. But for Normal, it had become an empty, meaningless phrase.

In Revelation 2, Jesus began his messages to the churches in Asia Minor. He addressed the church in Ephesus first. He commended their faithful service and doctrinal purity. However, Jesus also had a complaint. One thing was causing their light to flicker. In fact, it was in danger of burning out. Jesus warned, "You have left your first love" (Rev. 2:4). Though they believed right and were busy serving, they went wrong in their relationship. They had abandoned their love relationship with their best friend, Jesus.

This was Normal's condition, and it was the condition of the Ephesian Christians at the end of the first century A.D. It is also the condition of many Christians and churches in our day. How about you? How is your love relationship with Jesus? Do you need personal revival?

APPLICATION

1. Set aside some quiet time to evaluate your friendship with Jesus.
2. Are you living in the reality of Jesus as your best friend?
3. What evidence in your life demonstrates Jesus truly is your best friend?
4. What do you need to do right now about your love relationship with Jesus?

Chapter 20

FRESH

"Freshness" described the way Normal felt about his renewed relationship with Jesus Christ. He was amazed that he could slip into prayer almost without realizing it. He talked to the Lord about everything. Normal could not wait for opportunities to read the Bible, sit under sound teaching, or hear a good Biblical sermon. He loved giving testimony of how he came to faith in Christ and of his renewed walk with the Lord. Every aspect of his Christian walk was fresh.

As time passed he became concerned about maintaining the freshness. He went to see his pastor. The pastor gave Normal two key words: feelings and filling. Remember the pastor's train illustration? Believers can choose to place their faith in biblical facts rather than in personal feelings. Let's take another look at the illustration and personalize it.[1]

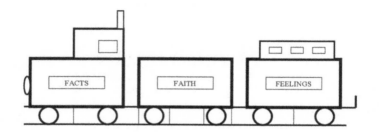

The train track represents the path to a growing, fresh relationship with Jesus Christ. The FAITH car represents your response to Jesus. The engine represents Biblical FACTS—Jesus is God, virgin born in a human body. He demonstrated His love for you when He was punished on the cross for the sins you committed. He died, was buried, and rose again. He is now seated at the Father's right hand, and He sent the Holy Spirit to live His life through you. He is your best friend; He loves you at all times. These, and many others, are Bible FACTS. They are reality. They call you to place your FAITH in God-revealed FACTS.

Sometimes your FEELINGS follow your FAITH in the FACTS, like a little red caboose. Sometimes the caboose is missing. When the caboose is gone, you can

---

1. Based on The Train Diagram, *Handbook for Christian Maturity* written by Bill Bright. Copyright 1982, 2007 Campus Crusade for Christ Inc. All rights reserved. Used by permission.

continue to focus your FAITH on the FACTS of God's Word. As you trust God's FACTS, rather than your FEELINGS, you will continue to grow in your walk with Jesus—feelings or no feelings.

The second key word Normal learned from Pastor Goodman was, "filling." Once again, we can personalize the message presented to Normal. You can follow the command of Ephesians 5:18. "And do not be drunk with wine, in which is dissipation; but be filled with the Spirit." Don't allow any substance to control you. Live every moment in continuous submission to Jesus' Lordship. Yield your life to the Holy Spirit's control. His Spirit will fill you, empower you, guide you, comfort you, keep you fresh, and use you in the lives of others. You will experience personal revival.

APPLICATION

1. Take some time to evaluate your own walk. Is "fresh" an accurate description your relationship with Jesus?"

2. Are you concerned about keeping your relationship "fresh" and growing?

3. Do you tend to put your trust in feelings or facts?

4. Are you trusting your strength to keep your walk with Jesus fresh, or are you submitting to Him, trusting the Holy Spirit to fill/control you?

Chapter 21

FRUITFUL

Our Lord Jesus said, "Abide in Me, and I in you. As the branch cannot bear fruit of itself, unless it abides in the vine, neither can you, unless you abide in Me. I am the vine, you *are* the branches. He who abides in Me, and I in him, bears much fruit; for without Me you can do nothing" (John 15:4-5).

Normal's fresh relationship with Jesus produced fruit. The closer he walked with the Lord, the more he impacted others. For the first time in his Christian life, Normal understood the relationship between abiding in Christ and bearing fruit. Fruit bearing was not a project for him to perform; it was the by-product of abiding.

Believers often struggle with bearing spiritual fruit. They want the Lord to use them. They want to make a difference in others' lives. They want to win the lost and encourage the found. However, guilt and dissatisfaction plagues many believers. Instead of "*much fruit*," they bear *minimal fruit*. Their connection to the vine is sure, but the harvest is pitiful.

What can a guilty, dissatisfied believer do? First, deal with the guilt. Confess your sin. God's promise remains true. "If we confess [agree with God about] our sins, He is faithful and just to forgive us our sins and to cleanse us from all unrighteousness" (1 John 1:9). He will forgive and cleanse any sin and every sin because "the blood of Jesus Christ His Son cleanses us from all sin" (v. 7). Trust His promise, His sacrifice, and His faithfulness, and your guilt will be gone.

Second, deal with the dissatisfaction. The most important thing a believer can do is focus on his or her first love—Jesus Christ. As a believer's personal walk with Jesus grows, things begin to happen. If you truly "abide in Christ," He will use you. Like Normal, you'll encourage saints and evangelize sinners. As your walk with Jesus grows, the things that are important to Him become important to you. You'll join Him in His business of saving sinners and building believers. The more you're around Him, the more you'll be like Him.

APPLICATION

1. Honestly evaluate your fruitfulness.
2. Are you trying to bear fruit in your own strength or out of guilt?

3. When you see a lack of fruitfulness in your life, how do you respond? Do you try harder, or do you revisit your personal walk with Jesus?

4. Spend some time reflecting on John 15:4-5. What can you accomplish without Jesus?

5. What is the most important thing you can do to ensure fruitfulness for God?

Chapter 22

MENTORING

In the weeks following Normal's "Friend Day," Normal enjoyed a close, growing relationship with his Best Friend. His family followed his lead. Average, Moody, and Happy developed a growing friendship with Jesus Christ as well. And that led to a nagging concern.

Looking back, Normal realized his spiritual journey had been like a roller coaster ride. There had been highs and lows. He experienced several spiritual highs, but the highs never lasted. During special services and various spiritual emphasis events at their church, he had dedicated himself to spiritual growth, evangelism, fasting and prayer, Bible study, and others. He had framed covenants and signed pledges, workbooks and guidebooks. He had rededicated his life to Christ at various times, thinking, "This time, things will be different." But it never was. The spiritual roller coaster went downhill much faster than it went up. Normal's rededications all returned to business as usual.

Eventually, Normal simply exited the ride. He told Pastor Goodman, "I embraced a bland, mediocre Christian life, but I didn't know it. I wasn't trying to stay indifferent. I was trying not to be disappointed. Now I'm wondering if I'm over-excited again, headed for another fizzle and failure. I don't want to end up deflated and defeated again."

Normal was afraid he would disappoint his family and disillusion those to whom he had witnessed. That concern took him to his pastor's office.

Pastor Goodman understood the concern. He had personal experience on the spiritual roller coaster. He encouraged Normal with a simple but profound, eye-opening lesson about Biblical facts, Christ-focused faith, and personal feelings. Normal wondered how he had missed the simple truth. He suspected he had missed other truths along the way as well. So, he asked his pastor to meet with him once a month to help him stay on the spiritual growth track.

Pastor Goodman agreed to the meetings on two conditions. First, Normal had to agree to complete all assigned homework before each meeting. Second, Normal had to be willing to mentor another man. The pastor called it "the Second Timothy 2:2 principle." The verse says, "The things you have heard from me, among many witnesses, commit to faithful men who will teach others also."

The Apostle Paul introduced Timothy to a simple mentoring process: be a learner; share what you have learned. The focus was not on a program but on relationships. By following Paul, Timothy became one of his most trusted co-workers. He commended Timothy to the church at Philippi.

> [19] But I trust in the Lord Jesus to send Timothy to you shortly, that I also may be encouraged when I know your state. [Timothy would report the condition of the Philippi church back to Paul.] [20] For I have no one like-minded, who will sincerely care for your state. [Timothy was unique. He wasn't a critic or a gossip looking for something bad to tell. He thought like his mentor. He genuinely wanted the best for the believers.] [21] For all seek their own, not the things which are of Christ Jesus. [22] But you know his proven character [How did Timothy become the mature, dependable believer?], that as a son with his father [He learned from Paul.] he served with me in the gospel [He shared what he learned with others.]" (Phil. 2:19-22).

This simple process works today. It is still God's plan for His church. It is still God's plan for discipleship.

Are you faithful, available, and teachable? Ask God to bring a mature friend into your life who will share what God has taught him or her. (By the way, men should mentor men and women should mentor women.) But don't stop the process. Also, ask God to bring a less mature believer into your life. Share what you have learned and are learning with that believer. Grow in grace together.

"The 2 Timothy 2:2 principle" is God's plan for the church. When I was a pastor, I practiced the principle; I regularly mentored men in my church. When God called me to lead in founding Northeastern Baptist College, our founding team made the 2 Timothy 2:2 principle the heartbeat of our mission statement. It declares:

> Our mission is to impact New England, the United States, and the World by training students to have **The Mind of a Scholar**, **The Heart of a Shepherd**, and **The Perseverance of a Soldier** through the provision of an accredited college education with a Biblical Foundation and a unique blend of Academic Excellence and Practical Mentoring.

From our first week of classes onward, we have put the 2 Timothy 2:2 principle into practice. To fulfill the "practical mentoring" portion of our mission statement, every student at Northeastern Baptist College participates in a weekly shepherding group. The groups are led by professors, and consist of no more than 12 students. The groups meet weekly for fellowship and spiritual encouragement. We also trust that one on one mentoring will grow out of these groups: professors mentoring students, and students mentoring other students.

Every believer needs a mentor in his or her life. In addition, every believer can mentor someone else.

In our parable, Pastor Goodman began mentoring Normal. In the process, Normal was willing for God to send another man into his life who needed to know the things he was learning from his pastor. Part One concluded with Typical recognizing Normal's spiritual growth, and realizing his own need for mentoring. Normal responded to Typical's request by saying, "I'd be honored. But I have two requirements..." Normal practiced the 2 Timothy 2:2 principle.

How about you?

Application

1. Do you have a spiritual mentor who encourages your relationship with Jesus? If not, pray for one right now. Be faithful, available, and teachable.

2. Are you a spiritual mentor? If so, encourage the one you mentor to pass on what you are teaching. You may need to require it as a condition of your mentoring, just as Pastor Goodman required of Normal, and Normal required of Typical.

3. If you are not a mentor, ask the Lord to bring a faithful, available, and teachable person of your gender into your life. You can be a spiritual men-

tor, a disciple maker. You can share what you are learning.

4. A final word. Mentoring is not a program to follow; it is a relationship to foster—a relationship with Jesus Christ. Jesus is your Best Friend. Introduce Him to someone else.

Appendix

YOU CAN KNOW FOR CERTAIN, HEAVEN IS YOUR HOME

On Sunday evening, June 3, 1984, I was operating the sound system at First Southern Baptist Church, Pueblo, Colorado. My pastor, Roy Spannagel, said, "We have no idea what will happen this week. Last Sunday we had no idea a 24 year old member of our congregation would die before we met again in this sanctuary." The 24 year old was a teacher and coach at a local high school. As far as anyone knew, he was the picture of health. However, he died suddenly and unexpectedly. He had a massive, fatal heart attack on the baseball field.

When the service ended, I visited with some friends before heading home. As I walked up to the front porch of our house, the door opened. My brother-in-law said, "Mark, you better get to the hospital. They had to take Mom in by ambulance."

I was 16 years old. As I drove to the hospital, I had a strong sense that Mom would never come home. Early the next morning, with most of her children singing praise songs outside her hospital room, she slipped into eternity.

My thoughts often return to those two weeks in the spring of 1984. Pastor Roy's words are forever etched in my memory: "We have no idea what will happen this week." It never crossed my mind that, at that moment, the unexpected was happening to my Mom, my family, and me.

A 100-year-old man said, shortly before he died, "I can't believe it all went by so fast." Life is short.

- The 24-year-old coach. Gone.
- The 60-year-old mother. Gone.
- The 100-year-old man. Gone.

Ready or not, life is short. Perhaps it was Capt. Obvious who said, "The latest statistics indicate that one of one dies."

We will all slip out of this life, into eternity. And you may be next.

Good News

Do you know for sure if you were to die today you would immediately go to Heaven to spend eternity with

Jesus? If not, I have good news for you. *You can know, without any doubt, that Heaven is your home.*

How?

It starts with understanding that *God loves you.*[1] He made you to have a real, vibrant, personal relationship with Him.

Second, *God is totally righteous.* The Bible says, "God is light and in Him is no darkness at all."[2] This means He is perfect and never does anything wrong. We, on the other hand, are just the opposite, which is the third vital truth.

Bad News

We are not righteous. The Bible says, "All have sinned and come short of the glory of God."[3]

Fourth, *sin will be punished.* God's holiness demands it and our sin earns it.

Death is the punishment for sin. "The wages [what we earn] of sin is death."[4] This death is not only physical; it is also spiritual. It results in spending all of eternity separated from God in a place of torment. The Bible calls that place, "The Lake of Fire."[5]

---

1. John 3:16
2. 1 John 1:5
3. Romans 3:23
4. Romans 6:23
5. Revelation 20:11-15

Good News?

So where is the good news? In spite of your sin, *God loves you and wants to have a personal relationship with you.* The Bible says, "For God so loved the world that He gave His only begotten Son, that whoever believes in Him should not perish but have everlasting life." The Father sent His Son—Jesus the Christ.

Jesus came, lived a perfect life, and died, accepting the punishment for OUR sins. He paid the price for all the wrong we have done, are now doing, or will do. The Bible says, "All we like sheep have gone astray [it's our natural tendency], everyone has turned to his own way [instead of God's way], but the LORD [the Father] laid on Him [Jesus] the sin of us all."[6]

The story doesn't end there. *Jesus rose from the dead, defeating sin, death, and the grave.* The Bible says, "Christ died for our sins according to the Scriptures, ... He was buried, and ... He rose again the third day according to the Scriptures."[7]

The Offer

He now offers forgiveness of all sin, a personal *relationship* with God in this life, and the absolute assurance of *Heaven* as your eternal home. He makes this offer to everyone.

6. Isaiah 53:6
7. 1 Corinthians 15:3-4

The question is, *"Have YOU taken Him up on His offer?"* The way you do so is very simple.

Jesus said, "He who believes in Me has everlasting life."[8] To believe on Jesus means to *turn away* [that's repentance] from trusting in your own ability to earn a relationship with God and gain a place in Heaven. It means to turn to Jesus, trusting Him, and Him alone [that's faith], for your salvation. You can turn to Jesus. You can trust Him right now. *You can have the free gift of eternal life.*

God said, *"Whoever calls* on the name of the LORD shall be saved."[9] Will you call on Him now? Below is a sample prayer. You don't have to say these exact words. Simply turn to Jesus in faith.

Dear Jesus,

I know I have sinned. I do not deserve a relationship with you, but I believe You love me. I believe You are God; You lived a perfect life, died in my place, and rose from the dead. Right now, I turn to You, trusting You to forgive me, to give me a real relationship with You, and to give me an eternal home in Heaven.

Thank you, Jesus, Amen.

If you trusted Jesus, you have eternal life. Welcome to God's Forever Family. Jesus will never leave

---

8. John 6:47
9. Romans 10:13

you. Now, Jesus is Your Best Friend, and He will love you at all times. You can grow in your relationship with Him.

Begin reading the book of John in the Bible. Check the table of contents if you can't find it. It is the 4th book of the New Testament part of the Bible.

Participating in a local, Bible-believing church will enhance your growth. Visit such a church as soon as possible. Speak with the Pastor. Tell him about your decision to trust Jesus. He will help you get on the right track of growing as a believer.

If you need help finding a Bible believing church in your area, we want to help you. You can visit us on the web at http://www.nebcvt.org. Call or send an email. We will help you find a church home.

ABOUT THE AUTHORS

Mark H. Ballard, faithful pastor, diligent church planter, passionate evangelist, innovative educator, creative and prolific author, pacesetting Baptist leader, is the husband of Cindy and dad of Benjamin. He graduated Criswell College with his Bachelor's, and Southeastern Baptist Theological Seminary with his M.Div. and PhD. Dr. Ballard, a native of Colorado, serves as the founding president of Northeastern Baptist College in Bennington, Vermont, and as a member of the Conservative Baptist Network Steering Council. Prior to launching NEBC, he served as a church planter and pastor in New Hampshire, Virginia, Florida, North Carolina, and Texas. Mark has filled pulpits, held revival services, and served as a conference speaker in numerous states for more than 30 years.

Timothy K. Christian serves as Adjunct Professor of Theology at Northeastern Baptist College and as Senior Pastor at Stamford Baptist Church in Stamford, Connecticut. Prior to this assignment, Dr. Christian served as a professor and administrator at Mid-America Baptist Theological Seminary. Dr. Christian also served as a pastor, transitional pastor, conference speaker, contributing editor, and co-author of several works. Tim is married to his lifelong friend and partner Judy. They have two married children, and seven grandchildren.

Other Books by Mark H. Ballard and Timothy K. Christian

Open Doors: The Pathway to God-Sized Assignments is an exciting account of God's supernatural activity. God opens doors—mega doors. He works mightily in, and for, those who see His doors and walk through by faith. Using faithful biblical exposition and inspiring personal illustrations, *Open Doors* invites you to join what God alone can do.

Priorities: Reaching the life God Intended is written to help you discover and accomplish your God-given priorities. In its pages, you will learn a simple process drawn from Ballard's practical expositions of Haggai. This process will guide you to use rather than lose your time. *Priorities* will help you invest your talents and treasures wisely and effectively.

Words Matter: What Is the Gospel? is an in-depth look into what the Gospel is, and just as importantly, what it is not. While the term "Gospel" has often been co-opted in an attempt to add to its message, the simple fact is the Gospel has one meaning: Christ crucified and risen again to take the penalty for our sins. In *Words Matter*, you will learn how important the Gospel truly is, and how it can transform your life eternally.